FOOTPRINTS

of the

1/4th Leicestershire Regiment

The Crossing of the Canal de St. Quentin at Bellenglise by the 46th (North Midland) Division, September, 1918.

(*Reproduced by kind permission of the Committee of the United Service Club*). Drawing by J. P. BEADLE.

FOOTPRINTS

of the

1/4th Leicestershire Regiment

AUGUST 1914 to NOVEMBER 1918

By JOHN MILNE

(Captain late 4th Battalion the Leicestershire Regiment)

With a Foreword by FIELD-MARSHAL LORD MILNE, G.C.B.,
G.C.M.G., D.S.O., D.C.L., LL.D., at one time an officer on
the General Staff of the North Midland Division, and Chief of
the Imperial General Staff, 1926-1933.

Illustrated from actual photographs.

Published for Past and Present Members
of the 4th Leicestershire Regiment by

EDGAR BACKUS, 44-46, CANK STREET
LEICESTER
1935.

Dedicated with the greatest affection and respect to
The Honorary Colonel of the 4th Leicestershire
Regiment,

COLONEL J. E. SARSON, C.B., O.B.E., V.D.,
T.D., D.L.

whose services with Volunteer and Territorial
Battalions of the Leicestershire Regiment cover a
period of 75 years.

Author's Note

I WISH TO TENDER MY SINCERE THANKS TO ALL THOSE
WHO HAVE HELPED ME TO WRITE THIS BOOK. THEIR
NAME IS LEGION.

JOHN MILNE.

Armistice Day, 1934.

FOREWORD

My only valid reason for venturing to write a foreword to this history is that, on the inauguration of the Territorial Army, I was posted to the staff of the North Midland Division, of which the 4th Battalion Leicestershire Regiment formed a part. With this division I spent two very pleasant years, during which time I learned to appreciate the potential value as soldiers of the men of the Midlands.

This appreciation was fully confirmed by the deeds and actions recounted in this book, which, though written primarily for those who served or whose relatives served in the battalion, will still, through its vivid description of the daily intimate and domestic life of an infantry unit, help the student reader to realise one aspect of the Great War.

Official histories may describe and explain great events and far-reaching movements with their reasons, causes and results; but, to fully understand these causes and results, something more human is required, viz., the knowledge of the influence of daily events on the body and mind of the fighting man, who in the end turns ideas into action. The following pages portray this picture, which, though at times far from a pleasant one, is always true. As you read you will realise the nerve-racking strain of the early years of trench warfare. You may feel inclined to say :— Why this unnecessary delay ? Why all these apparently useless losses ? It is the means available, not the wishes of the Commanders, which in the end direct the course of battle, and if you, employing only the means then available, can suggest any other method of avoiding trench warfare, you will have succeeded where the best brains on both sides failed. Irresponsible criticism is always easy.

In the latter half of the book the writer pictures the great battles again from the point of view of the fighting man. Bored with the deadly monotony but comparative safety of trench warfare, he welcomes with the exhilarating enthusiasm of youth the tenfold more dangerous task of active fighting, where "the sights are sickening, the noise appalling and the discomfort intense." Under devastating shell fire, the youth of Leicestershire went forward at the call of duty and, as you read, pride of race and country will make your heart beat faster and your blood pulsate more rapidly. If it doesn't it ought to. The younger generation may well be proud of their fathers. Those who have never done anything for their country are always ready to vilify the soldier, but dare they emulate the life and conduct of a man like the late Lt.-Col. B. W. Vann, V.C., M.C., 6th Sherwoods, who fell at Ramicourt—clergyman—soldier—hero, and there were many like him.

At the beginning of the war many difficulties had to be overcome, and whilst it is usual to blame the professional soldiers for the delinquencies, it must always be remembered that the losses of 1914 had left only a handful to organise and train a national army ten times the size of the original Expeditionary Force ; the fault lay with the leaders of the nation, who scornfully resisted adequate preparation for war during peace.

As a picture of modern war, of its horrors and beastliness and of the courage and nobility of the fighters, I recommend this book to all readers willing to face facts.

MILNE,
F.M.

Contents

List of Illustrations

List of Maps

OFFICERS OF THE 1/4th LEICESTERSHIRE REGIMENT AT LUTON, IN OCTOBER, 1914

2/Lt. G. E. F. Russell   2/Lt. J. F. Johnson   2/Lt. W. N. Dunn   Lt. G. A. Brogden, R.A.M.C.   2/Lt. F. M. Waite
2/Lt.   Lt.   Lt.   Lt.   2/Lt.   Lt.   Lt. & Q.M.
H. F. Papprill   J. G. Abell   W. B. Jarvis   Capt. & Adjt.   G. J. Harvey   H. C. Brice   F. S. Parr   A. E. Ball
        Capt.   Maj.   Lt.-Col.   R. S. Dyer-Bennet   T. P. Fielding-Johnson   J. C. Baines   H. Haylock
       A. C. Cooper   L. V. Wykes   W. A. Harrison   Capt.   Capt.
2/Lt.   Capt.   G. J. Harvey
M. B. Douglas   Lt. T. Whittingham   2/Lt. A. C. Clarke   2/Lt. R. C. Harvey   2/Lt. L. Forsell
    Capt.
R. A. Faire   B. F. Newill

Nominal Roll of Officers of 4th Leicestershire Regiment who originally embarked at Southampton for foreign service on dates shown (taken from War Diary 4.Leic.R.).

Lt.-Col. W. A. Harrison, T.D.   2.3.15

Major L. V. Wykes   „
   „   J. A. Potter   „

Capt. A. C. Cooper   „   k. in a.   16.5.15
  „   T. P. Fielding-Johnson   „
  „   B. F. Newill   4.3.15
  „   H. Haylock   2.3.15   k. in a.   10.5.15
  „   L. Corah   „   k. in a.   13.10.15
  „   J. Milne   „
  „   R. A. Faire   „   k. in a.   13.10.15

Lieut. W. B. Jarvis, T.O.   4.3.15
  „   G. J. Harvey   „
  „   F. N. Tarr, M.G.O.   2.3.15   k. in a.   18.7.15
  „   J. G. Abell, Telephone O.   4.3.15
  „   F. S. Parr, Res. M.G.O.   2.3.15
  „   T. Whittingham, Scout O.   „   k. in a. 13.10.15
  „   H. C. Brice   „   died of w. 10.6.15

2nd-Lt. A. C. Clarke   4.3.15   k. in a.   9.5.15
  „   L. Forsell, Res. T.O.   „
  „   R. C. Harvey   2.3.15   k. in a. 13.10.15
  „   F. M. Waite   „   k. in a.   7.6.15
  „   K. Dalgliesh   „
  „   J. F. Johnson   „   k. in a. 13.10.15
  „   G. E. F. Russell   „   k. in a. 13.10.15
  „   M. B. Douglas   „
  „   H. F. Papprill   „
  „   W. N. Dunn   4.3.15

Capt. & Adj. R. S. Dyer-Bennet (Leic. Regt.)
       2.3.15
Lieut. G. A. Brogden, R.A.M.C. (T.)
       2.3.15
Lieut. & Q.M. A. E. Ball   „

We are the Leicester Boys.   We are the Leicester Boys.
We know our manners.   We spend our tanners.
We are respected wherever we go.
When you see us on parade open the windows wide,
All the girls begin to cry, "I tiddly, I tiddly, I ti, ti."
We are the Leicester Boys.

(Marching song of the 4th Leicesters.   Author unknown.)

CHAPTER I

MOBILISATION

THE sun of August 5th, 1914, shone pleasantly on the Magazine Gateway at Leicester. It was a beautiful day.

From the Magazine Square there issued, now and then, a squad of men in khaki. Rather more people than usual were standing about the street, otherwise everything outwardly seemed normal.

But the atmosphere was charged with excitement; the people felt and looked awestruck; they were wondering what would happen next, what would be required of them, and why such a disturbance should be launched on their peace-loving lives. War with Germany was declared, and now for the first time the eyes of the whole town were turned on things military in general, and the Leicestershire Territorial units in particular.

The War Office had telegraphed the magic words "Mobilise Troopers" and the Regular and Auxiliary Forces of Great Britain sprang to arms.

There was much stir at the Magazine in an upper room hung with pictures and photographs which dated from the early days of the Volunteers. There was the Colonel (Lt.-Col. W. A. Harrison, T.D.) who had served in the South African War, there was the Adjutant (Capt. R. S. Dyer-Bennet) who came from the Regular Battalion, and in and out came Majors, Captains, Subalterns. In and out limped Major Serjeantson, Secretary of the Territorial Association, advising, answering questions, giving all manner of help. Waiting about stood boys who had just left Public Schools, and were seeking vacant commissions. Up and down the stone steps ran Orderly Room Sergeant, and Clerk, Sergeant-Major, and Quartermaster very full of bustle with papers in hand. On an oblong table in the centre of the room lay mobilisation orders, in red paper covers to which a white label proclaiming them secret was attached. This was the Headquarters of the 4th Leicestershire Regiment.

The eight companies of the battalion (the four company formation had not then been extended to the Territorial Force) mobilised in eight different Board Schools in the town, and the process of bringing them from a peace to a war footing went on daily. Clothing, necessaries and equipment were issued. Recruits were drafted in from the National Reserve, most of whom were old soldiers, who were either too old or unfit to march in full equipment, and many of them were discharged a day or two after drawing their Bounty of five pounds. Nominal

I

rolls were made out, and all the army forms which are necessary to make the private soldier what he is were filled in. There was plenty to do, and progress had to be reported at the Magazine twice daily by Officers Commanding Companies.

The Transport Section were even busier than the rest of the battalion. Horses were requisitioned, and also wagons, and half-a-dozen bakers' carts for carrying ammunition. Very little was done in the way of medical inspections, which was a pity, and bayonets were not sharpened, which did not matter.

At last orders were received to proceed to Belper.

On August 12th the afternoon sun blazed down on the empty Magazine Square. It was one of the hottest days of the year. A company of the 4th marched in through the gates, formed into line, halted and stood at ease; one by one the remaining companies marched in and took up their position in quarter column. The men were dressed in Field Service Marching Order, and were each carrying 100 rounds of ammunition, no light burden for those used only to the factory and office; but their hearts were in the right place, and they felt that there was a life of adventure before them as they leaned on their rifles and mopped the sweat from their faces.

There were a lot of spectators in the Magazine Square. They were the friends and relations of officers and men, who had come to see them march away. The Duchess of Rutland was among them, for the Marquis of Granby was a subaltern in the battalion, and the Duke of Rutland was its Honorary Colonel.

Suddenly there is a sharp word of command; the Colonel comes on parade, the bayonets are fixed, and the arms brought to the "present." The Colours and Colour Party, and a large escort, march to Saint Martin's Church to lay up the colours while the battalion is away on active service. A thrill passes through the ranks and through the spectators. The heat of the day is forgotten; the weight of the packs and the ammunition seems suddenly to vanish. There is only one thought in everybody's mind—"The Colours."

Why is it that the Colours send a mysterious trickle down the spine of every soldier? Is it because the soul of every man serving or who has served with the regiment is in some way embodied in the Colours? Never mind what it is, there is something sacred, mysterious, and thrilling about these pieces of rich silk embroidered with gold and silver thread. One thing is certain—they are alive. Caesar knew it, Napoleon knew it, and the 4th Leicestershires know it now as they bid a silent farewell to the Colours so many of them will never see again.

This is the first time many members of the battalion have left their homes for any long period, and leave-taking is not an easy matter; later in the war they will get more used to saying "good-bye," but to-day there is an uncomfortable lump in the throat, the sun is uncomfortably hot, they will be glad when the battalion moves off.

The Colour Party return and the battalion marches down Newarke Street; the factory windows are crowded, the streets are full. There is a group of elderly gentlemen on the steps of the Leicestershire Club; they are employers of some of the men in the ranks; they look and they wonder; they wonder what will be the end of it all.

The battalion marches on; it does not march well; the ranks are augmented by elderly men from the National Reserve, many of whom have not marched for a long time and are thoroughly out of condition. F.S.M.O. is heavy, the day is very hot, the crowd is distracting. At the bottom of Belvoir Street it is very thick, and right up Granby Street to the Midland Station people swarm round the troops shouting farewell to their sons, sweethearts and friends; shouting to anyone and everyone, for in this time of crisis everyone speaks to his neighbour. An old, dirty-looking, motherly woman accosts a young officer as he marches in front of his company into the station. "I shall be waiting for you when you come back, me duck," she cries. He has never seen her before, and hopes he never will again, but the words stick in his memory.

The battalion entrains for Belper on No. 1 platform; the men throw their equipment on the racks, unbutton their collars and fight for the windows. The doors slam, the guard waves his green flag, a cheer goes up as the train steams out of the station, and the 4th Leicestershires leave their native town praying that they may get to France before the war is over.

And the elderly gentlemen at the Leicestershire Club walk slowly down its steps to their business, still wondering what will be the end of it all.

CHAPTER II

TRAINING

THE battalion remained at Belper only a few days; it was quartered in schools and empty factories, and the time was spent in route marching and volunteering for service abroad.

From Belper, with the rest of the Lincoln and Leicester Brigade, the battalion was ordered to Luton, in the area where the whole of the North Midland Division T.F. was to assemble. This entailed marching into Derby on a Saturday night, but even after the few days training the men were in much better fettle, and they swung along the road singing, "Who, Who, Who's Your Lady Friend?" and "When the Beer Is on the Table I'll Be There."

It was a fine summer evening, and all the village maidens turned out to see the show, and a lot of handkerchief waving and ogling went on ; but when the battalion got to Derby the populace turned out en masse. There was shouting and cheering from the crowd, all sorts of remarks were passed by the onlookers who were of all classes and ages and who were seeing to it that Derby gave a hearty welcome to the troops. But one old man, who was really very drunk and who was staggering along the pavement, could only shout "God bless you, boys" which seemed to be the most sensible sentiment expressed by the whole throng.

At 8 p.m., after a twelve-mile march, the place of entrainment was reached. It was a goods siding, but the battalion did not entrain until 3 a.m., owing to the brilliance of either the railway company or the Staff. The time was spent in a field and the men were very chilled by the night air. Some good church people served tea in a tin church hut which was close by. This was very much appreciated by all ranks, and was one of the many kind actions done by civilians during the War without reward or notice, which emanated from sheer kindness of heart and for which the troops were truly thankful.

On arrival at Luton the men were billeted in various places, some in private houses, some in schools and chapels. The people of Luton were very kind to the troops, and gave them as good accommodation as possible, and were soon firm friends with the men billeted on them.

At Luton and St. Albans the whole North Midland Division began serious training. Their commander, Major-General Stuart-Wortley, was not only most anxious to get his division to France, but he wanted it to be the first Territorial division to

4

get there, and he spent a great deal of time on the steps of the War Office asking for embarkation orders.

Training intensively for war is hard work, especially in hot weather, but the battalion quickly improved in efficiency in spite of the constant changes in personnel, due to the arrival of new drafts of recruits and the weeding out of unfit, home service and unsuitable men.

The fact that men were in billets made discipline difficult, but by the end of October there was a general feeling in the division that it was fit to take the field, and there is no doubt that if it had been sent overseas at that time it would have given an excellent account of itself.

While at Luton the division was inspected by General Sir Ian Hamilton, and also by Lord Kitchener, who was overheard to say to General Stuart-Wortley, as he inspected the battalion, that the division could not go abroad until its second line division was ready to take its place at home.

After the inspection the division marched past in column and quarter column. What a sight it is, a glittering sea of bayonets, wave after wave of sombre khaki, battalion after battalion, brigade after brigade, interspersed with well-mounted commanding officers, spruce keen-eyed adjutants, waxed-moustached sergeant-majors looking exceeding fierce. The cream of the manhood of the Midlands are here, big sunburnt men, all fighting fit. They are well turned out, the packs are square, the puttees neat, the rifles spotless. They handle their arms with soldierly precision; they march past like a moving wall. The park at Luton Hoo echoes with strident words of command, the marching of men, the plodding of hooves, and the rattle of harness and gun wheels. A division at war strength is an awe-inspiring and wonderful sight at any time, but in war time with every man with the glint of battle in his eyes, and straining at the leash to get to grips with his country's foes, it is a sight only for the gods. This is, of course, from the spectators' point of view.

In the ranks things are quite different. Reveille has been half-an-hour earlier. The inspection on the company parade ground has been more unpleasant than usual ; the empty water-bottle of Private Buggins has caused the company commander to use words of imprecation new even to some of the sergeants. The adjutant has been exceedingly curt with some of the subalterns, who have retaliated on the lance-corporals (unpaid). The Colonel's mare has been fidgety, a thing which always upsets the C.O., and the second-in-command has been more officious than is his wont.

So, having been under arms for four-and-a-half hours, the battalion marches past in quarter column, a seething mass of suppressed profanity, stifled curses and ejaculations such as

"By the right," "Dress back on the left," "Press on your butt" and "For God's sake get into step." The men in the ranks jostle one another, elbows delve into ribs and toes are trodden on, but everybody is trying his best and by dint of perspiration, blasphemy, and united effort the battalion effects the wheel in quarter column and all the other required evolutions, and then it marches home thoroughly tired, but satisfied that it has put up a good show for K. of K.

His Majesty the King also inspected the division, but, on the day arranged for the original inspection, there was a prolonged downpour of rain. The troops paraded, however, but after a good deal of standing about the parade was postponed to later in the week, and the troops marched home singing in the rain.

It is a curious phenomenon in the British Army this singing in the rain. Often on fine days the column marches silently, but directly the rain begins out come the mouth organs, everybody whistles, everybody sings, though the rain is running down the waterproof sheets and the trousers and puttees are sodden.

The battalion enjoyed itself at Luton, the men got fat and sunburnt, the N.C.O.'s became spruce and efficient, the officers were within striking distance of Town, the transport mules became less recalcitrant, the band learned to play "Tipperary," and the inhabitants were distinctly friendly.

There was a good deal of drill, a lot of route marching up and down the New Bedford Road, there were outpost schemes at Chaul End, there was musketry on the new range, there were kit inspections and foot inspections, inoculations, church parade on Sundays, pay on Friday afternoons, there were long field days, and there was the Battle of Sundon, when the battalion stayed out all day and all night and arrived home with the milkman.

There was week-end leave, there was absence without leave, there was company office, there was battalion office at the gas works, there was confinement to barracks, which was difficult to enforce, there were rumours of German spies on motor-cycles, there were rumours of trainloads of Russians passing through Luton with snow on their boots, there was the George Hotel, and the Red Lion, and there was the daughter at the billet with the blue eyes and the sympathetic nature.

A lecture was given to all officers of the division by Mr. Miller MacGuire, a barrister, who was the author of books on strategy and military history. He gave a very interesting discourse on current events with references to the Russian steam roller. But he said that on the Western Front it looked as though it was going to be a war of attrition; he mentioned the word "attrition" at least ten times. Very few of those present realised what it meant, but a year later when they had lost most of their friends they began to understand its meaning.

Early in September the news came that Captain R. H. Olivier, who had been adjutant of the battalion until the end of 1913, had been killed in France while serving with his Regiment, the Duke of Cornwall's Light Infantry. Everybody was sorry, but nobody was surprised, as he was an officer of great dash and energy, a "thruster" in the best sense of the word, and one who would always be in the thick of the fight. He had seen a good deal of fighting in South and East Africa, and had kept his company together in the retreat from Mons, which is saying much. When adjutant, he was a strict disciplinarian, but the most popular officer in the battalion. It was to him and his predecessor, Captain B. J. Lang, that the battalion very largely owed the high standard of discipline, the capacity for hard work, and the wonderful esprit de corps which inspired all ranks and which has now hardened into tradition. Both these officers worked very hard instructing officers and N.C.O.'s and encouraging them to make themselves efficient for war service, and they were never tired of warning all ranks that war with Germany was perilously imminent. The battalion owes them a very great deal and their names should be always remembered.

In the small hours of Monday, November 16th, the battalion received orders to march at once to Ware, a distance of about 28 miles. The whole division was to move, and the battalion was to be ready by 8 a.m. This was short notice and kit had to be packed hurriedly, billets paid for and rations issued; however, the battalion was ready to move at the time ordered. It was an unpleasant day with showers of cold, driving rain; there were prolonged halts, without any order to fall out, due to transport and guns being held up in front through stiff hills, overloaded wagons, faulty harness and bad staff work. In some cases rations had not been issued, and the men became hungry as well as fatigued; however, they marched well and arrived at Ware about 7 p.m., having been under arms for the best part of twelve hours. It was a very long and tiring march, and will be long remembered by those who took part in it.

After a day's halt at Ware, the battalion moved to Bishops Stortford, a pleasant little Hertfordshire town. Here billeting accommodation was very varied. The officers were principally in private houses, the men in public houses, schools or the old Post Office. Training went on as usual. Field firing was carried out at Dunstable. The battalion began to get restless; surely it was now fit to go to France?

Christmas Day came, and the battalion paraded for service at the fine old Parish Church, and afterwards marched past the commanding officer; the band played the regimental march, cigarettes and tobacco were distributed at company headquarters, and after that anything happened.   The beer was on the table, the Checquers and the Star Inn echoed with revelry, the old Post Office rocked with mirth.   It was Christmas Day, it only came once a year, and it might not come again.

CHAPTER III

EMBARKATION

In the New Year equipment and stores of all kinds began to pour into Bishops Stortford from the ordnance, and after his second glass of port at mess the quartermaster (Lt. A. E. Ball) whispered confidentially to his subaltern friends, "You are really going this time." And they rejoiced exceedingly.

On February 19th, 1915, His Majesty the King inspected the North Midland Division in Great Hallingbury Park. The infantry marched past eight abreast, the subalterns carrying rifles. The senior officers saluted, the men turned their head and eyes smartly towards their Sovereign, the band played martial music, the bayonets glistened, the adjutant looked pensive, the regimental sergeant-major looked suitably bellicose, and the transport rumbled by complete to the last buckle with the mules grinning in their new harness.

What a transformation from the battalion which left Leicester six months before ! Here was the complete fighting machine with every man trained, fit and longing to get to the Front. What efficiency, what discipline, what patriotism ! But no prophetic voice hurled from the moving ranks the ancient but appropriate greeting of the gladiators, "Ave Caesar, morituri te salutant."

After this things began to move quickly. On February 22nd a new brigadier arrived (Gen. J. W. Clifford) to take command of the Lincoln and Leicester Brigade, vice Brig.-Gen. A. W. Taylor. On February 25th a draft of fifty men arrived from the 2/4th Leicestershires to bring the battalion up to strength. Everybody was busy. Pay books were being made up and issued ; there were medical inspections, issues of new boots, and nominal rolls galore. The four company formation had just superseded the old eight company system, and there had been a lot of changing about in the battalion in consequence, and much extra office work as well.

At last everything was ready and on February 27th the battalion paraded to leave Bishops Stortford. It was a wet, cold morning and there was the usual standing about in the vicinity of the railway station while everything was loaded up. The battalion left in two trainloads.

There were a good many relations and friends present to say "good-bye." It was a sad business even to watch, as it was quite obvious that in a good many cases this was really "good-bye" and not "au revoir." A wife came with her daughter to see her

9

husband off; they all kissed and then he sat in the carriage waiting
for the train to start, and they waved to each other and smiled,
but by the look in their eyes one knew that they felt instinctively
that they would never see each other again.   And so it happened.

A certain lance-corporal was late for parade but he came along
to the station in plenty of time ; he had two women with him ;
one was his mother and the other was his wife whom he had
married only the day before.   He took his place in the ranks
and the company marched into the station and entrained.   Three
months later he was shot through the brain in a filthy little
trench on the Messines Ridge.

However, everybody was glad to leave Bishops Stortford,
though they had spent a very pleasant time there and had made
a great many friends ; but they were all glad that the time of
training was over, and that the time of testing had begun, and a
great wave of enthusiasm swept through the battalion.   All
felt that it was a great honour to form part of the first Territorial
division to go to France and take its place side by side with the
Regulars, the heroes of Mons, the veterans of the First Battle of
Ypres.   Every man realised that the reputation, not only of the
battalion and the division, but of the whole Territorial Army
was at stake, and all ranks were on their mettle.

Yes, everybody was glad to leave Bishops Stortford ; training
was getting very monotonous, all this saying "good-bye" got on
one's nerves, and it was very pleasant to sit back in the railway
carriage and think, "Well, anyway, that's over."   Everybody
was young, fit and full of beans, out for a great adventure, out
for a bit of fun, quite ready to die on the field of honour if really
necessary, quite ready to "wind up the watch on the Rhine."
Anyway, the spring was coming, so was the spring offensive,
and so was the rest of the Territorial Force, and Kitchener's
colossal army.   So there would be some toughish fighting, and
then the war would finish with a triumphal march to Berlin in
the summer, if not before.   And it would be rather jolly coming
home to Leicester after the Boches had been beaten, and telling
those other fellows who had not joined up what one really thought
of them.   Then someone looked out of the window and saw a
trainload of blue-coated wounded passing ; that rather brought
one down to earth, and the troop train rumbled into Southampton
Docks station and the men detrained.

Instead of going straight on board three nights were spent in
Southampton.   The men were distributed in schools, ware-
houses and the Southampton Rest Camp.   The officers were
quartered in the "Flowers Hotel" close to the docks.   Embarkation orders were hourly expected.   At last they came and half
the battalion embarked in the "Golden Eagle" and "Queen
Empress" on the afternoon of Tuesday, March 2nd.   Two

staff officers stood at the top of the gangway and counted the troops as they went on board, and then the men sat about the decks until dark when the boats sailed. As they left the docks there was a lot of cheering, it was a fine night, morale was high, the men were very pleased with themselves. Let the Allemands beware, the 4th Leicesters were coming. And so they slipped down the Solent, through the beams of the searchlights. The Channel was calm. It was going to be a good war.

The morning of March 3rd found headquarters and two companies of the battalion lying alongside the quay at Havre waiting to disembark. It was a fine bright day and everybody was in excellent spirits. Lots of the men had never before crossed the Channel, and they were very much interested in everything they saw when they disembarked and marched through the streets keeping well to the right of the road, which was in itself an innovation. They soon began to pick up some French and the first word they learned was "Estaminet." The people in the streets took little notice of the battalion as they had seen plenty of British troops before. So with wonder in their hearts and perspiration on their faces the 4th Leicesters marched four miles to No. 6 Infantry Rest Camp, which was on a hill just outside the town. Here they camped in tents, washed themselves at the troughs provided, and wrote home to say that their address was now B.E.F. France. All the letters had to be censored, and the supply of field postcards soon ran out.

There was an issue of goatskin coats, which were very welcome because the weather turned very cold and there was sleet and rain. They were really wonderful coats, all sorts of colours, and all smelling strongly of goat; but the men loved them and sounds of "baa baa" were heard all over the camp.

There was also an issue of socks, quite good socks too, though of all sorts and sizes; they came as a gift from "Queen Alexandra and the Women of the Empire." One or two of the brighter lads enquired from their quartermaster-sergeants whether they would also be recipients of gifts from the "Women of the Alhambra"; the answers they received were, of course, quite unprintable: quartermaster-sergeants were ever artists, and their language is always picturesque.

The officers spent some time unravelling the mysteries of the "Playfair Code" under the erudite tuition of the adjutant, and in strolling round the camp, where huts were being erected at a great pace.

Close by was Harfleur, which somehow seemed reminiscent of Henry the Fifth and Shakespeare; then there was a large valley, which was pointed out as being the place where four Uhlans were captured at the beginning of the war.

Divisional Orders were also read out on parade, in which it

was stated that certain private soldiers of certain Regular regiments had been tried by general court martial on certain dates for desertion, or sleeping at their post, and had been sentenced to be shot, and that the sentences had been duly carried out. This was extremely heartening for the troops.

CHAPTER IV

BEHIND THE LINES

On March 5th the "City of Dunkirk" with the other half of the battalion on board arrived at Havre. At 1.10 p.m. the whole battalion entrained at the Gare de Marchandises, thirty-eight men to a cattle truck, and the officers in second-class carriages. On the platform there was an excellent buffet with food and hot drinks; it was run by some English ladies and was a very great boon to all ranks.

The journey started at 2 a.m. and the destination was kept secret. It was a slow jolting business and nobody slept much. The rations consisted of bully beef (Fray Bentos), biscuits and jam; tea was supplied at one or two halts en route, when the men, very glad to stretch their legs, jumped out of the crowded wagons with straw in their hair and laughter on their lips; in fact, they seemed to treat the journey as a huge joke.

At 10.45 p.m. on March 6th the train pulled up in Cassel station and the news at once went round that the 5th Leicestershires were already in the trenches. This came as something of a surprise to those who had anticipated training behind the lines for a couple of months.

There was some confusion with regard to billets; it was very dark and drizzling with rain, but eventually everyone found shelter of some sort or other, but the staff work on this occasion could hardly be called brilliant.

Next day the battalion paraded at 10 a.m. It was Sunday, the church bells were ringing, and the peasants dressed mostly in black were going to Mass as usual. It was very cold, and the battalion marched to Zuytpeene, and went into billets at various farms. The officers lived in the farmhouses, and the men slept in the barns. There was a fall of snow and life altogether was bleak; the barns were draughty and the stone floors of the farms were cold and damp; anyone who got a bed was lucky.

Some of the Leicestershire Yeomanry were in the vicinity, and many of them visited the battalion. They had been in France since before Christmas, and so had plenty to say about life in the trenches and conditions generally.

On March 9th the battalion moved to Strazeele, a distance of about nine miles. The route was through Cassel and Caestre, where General Sir Horace Smith-Dorrien watched the battalion march by. The road was mostly hard cobbled pavé which was trying to march on, and, as every man's pack was crammed

13

full with just as much as he was able to carry, everybody was tired when Strazeele was reached at 2.40 p.m.

The battalion was again billeted in farms. The men were getting quite used to a nomadic life ; it was good experience, and everyone (even the stupid fellow) was beginning to realise that he had got to look after himself if he wanted to be comfortable. In the evening heavy firing was heard. The Battle of Neuve Chapelle had begun.

The next day the firing still continued and the battalion was under orders to move at an hour's notice. A parade in "fighting order" was held in the afternoon. It was quite obvious that there was "something doing," and that the battalion might shortly be in the firing line. For the moment, however, life was not strenuous and consisted of doing nothing, discussing the situation, and listening to the latest rumours.

It was at Strazeele that Field Punishment No. 1 was first awarded to a member of the battalion. It was not a pleasant sight to see a man tied up to a wagon wheel in front of his comrades ; in fact everybody hated it, but it made all ranks realise that war was a very different proposition to training at home. Still, within the sound of the guns, there seemed something ludicrous in tying up a fellow one day and expecting him, if necessary, to die cheerfully for his King and Country the next. But then war is full of grim jests.

At breakfast time on March 11th it was pretty certain that the battalion would move from Strazeele during the day, and it seemed likely that it would go into action as the sound of the bombardment still continued.

The "just before the battle, mother" feeling is a little uncomfortable and bewildering. There you sit in a cosy farmhouse with two or three other fellows, feeling as fit as a fiddle and eating an enormous breakfast of bacon and eggs and bread and jam ; the sun pours in at the windows, the birds are twittering to each other, Madame stands by the Dutch stove sucking her teeth and dispensing café au lait, the batmen are packing the valises, nothing unusual is happening but the rumble of gunfire in the distance ; and yet you have a disconcerting thought at the back of your brain that something nasty may befall during the next twenty-four hours, and that this may be the last breakfast some of you sitting there will eat. Yes, it certainly is a little uncomfortable, but anyway it does not last long, and the bacon and eggs are very good ; nothing like a full stomach; and after all what on earth did you come out for if it was not to fight ?

About noon orders to move reached the companies, and the battalion marched with the rest of the brigade to Sailly sur la Lys, a distance of about twelve miles.

Twelve miles in a motor-car on modern roads seems a very

short distance, but marching in column of fours over bad roads, with constant checks and halts, is a tedious business when carrying a pack on the back, a rifle on the shoulder, a full water-bottle and 100 rounds of ammunition. But on this occasion there was an element of excitement in it. The distant sound of the guns gradually getting nearer, the aeroplanes overhead, the little wooden crosses by the roadside marked "Unknown British Soldier. R.I.P.," the gunners wearing beards, and caps on which was scribbled "R.F.A." in indelible pencil in place of a badge. There was an optimistic cavalry trooper, who assured everybody during one of the halts that his major had told him quite definitely that this was the final break through and that the Germans were "packing up." There was a Canadian standing by the way who shouted :—"Is the Magazine still standing ?" and there was a voice from the ranks which promptly replied :—"Yes, and the Bell Hotel, too."

The afternoon passed, the long column still marched on, dusk came and then dark, but it was still marching ; at last it came to a halt in Sailly. The men were tired and hungry, and then suddenly from every cottage and alleyway Canadians appeared with tins full of biscuits, which they handed down the ranks. (Fine fellows, these Canadians, thought the battalion.) Parties of Regulars were seen going towards the firing line, and it was thought that the battalion might go straight into the line also, but instead it took over the billets of the Canadians. (Fine fellows, these Canadians, but somewhat erratic in their domestic usages, thought the battalion, as they cleared up the very odd contents of their billets.)

The Canadians referred to belonged to the 1st Canadian Division and, as every schoolboy knows, they saved the situation at the Second Battle of Ypres by tremendous sacrifice. They were a magnificent body of men, big fellows with hearts as large as elephants.

The battalion remained at Sailly for two days, during which time it was under orders to move at an hour's notice. A certain amount of alleged sniping went on at night, but nobody was hit. There was little to do all day except to watch aeroplanes being "archied," which was quite novel and exciting. The officers strolled up the road to see "Grandmother," the 15-inch howitzer, being fired. The same gun can now be seen in the Imperial War museum. A major of marines was in command of it, and it caused a lot of interest and made a lot of noise, and the gun's crew were full of the terrific amount of damage it had done to the targets it had selected in the German lines.

There was also an armoured train, which puffed up and down the railway line and fired occasionally. The news soon came through that our infantry were digging in, which was very disappointing, and it gradually began to be realised that there was little chance of breaking through the German line to any extent.

A lot of literature dealing with trench warfare was distributed containing useful hints about standing perfectly still if one happened to be in No Man's Land when a Verey light went up, and stating that trenches should be dug wide enough to allow the passage of a stretcher. Many sore feet had been caused through marching in new boots, and these were now carefully attended to. Motor buses arrived from Strazeele laden with the goatskin coats and officers' valises which had been left behind ; the men were glad to see the coats again as the nights were cold.

Much interest was aroused when a cottager went to a drain pipe by the side of the road in front of his dwelling and pulled out of it a Uhlan lance, which he had picked up during the German advance the previous year. But he took great care to put it back in its hiding place, not knowing when the Germans might recapture his village.

Sunday arrived (March 14th) and the companies held independent church parades. In the afternoon the battalion marched to the next village, Bac St. Maur, about a mile away, where it once more went into billets.

During the night heavy firing was heard and orders were received to "stand to." The Battle of St. Eloi was in progress and the Germans were attacking heavily. However, they were beaten off and the services of the 46th Division (as the North Midland was now called) were not required. On the 16th, the fighting having quietened down, the battalion was ordered to move to various farms in the neighbourhood of Steenwerck, a few miles away.

The Flemish farm in 1915 was probably much the same as the Flemish farm 200 years previously, and at both periods it was occupied by British soldiers.

There was the farmhouse with its stone floor, quite clean, but very cold and damp to sleep on ; there was the Dutch stove, which stood like a fortress at the end of the room, from which café au lait could always be procured at a moment's notice, and on which something was always cooking. There was Madame, the stout and portly custodian of the stove, in a white apron and felt bedroom slippers, with a wooden spoon in one hand and a pudding basin in the other. The stove was the centre of all the activities of the place ; it might have contained the sacred fire and Madame might have been one of the Vestal Virgins (though assuredly she was not) from the amount of attention she paid to it ; but then Madame paid attention to everything. She saw that the major had the most comfortable bed, she made an unimpeachable omelette for the company mess, she did a roaring trade in café au lait with the rank and file, she understood the

French of the quartermaster-sergeant, she warned her daughter against the blandishments of enterprising lance-corporals, she chained the big black dog into the wheel that churned the cream, she comforted her weeping hysterical neighbour who was half-demented by the war, and she tucked up the grinning telephone orderly in two chairs and a blanket before shuffling off to bed candle in hand. She ruled the household with a rod of iron, but it was the one with which she raked the stove.

Outside was the midden on which anything and everything was thrown ; it supported a few fowls, a pig or two wallowed in it, and occasionally private soldiers who walked across it suddenly found themselves up to their waists in filth, and had to be extricated by hilarious comrades with poles.

Then there were the barns where the men lived, slept, were fed, and were fed up. Some barns were better than others ; some were brick, some wooden and some were made of wood and mud combined ; all were draughty, most contained a certain amount of straw, which varied in quantity and freshness according to the "scrounging" abilities of the company quartermaster-sergeant. There were the usual rats, mice and lice, the beams were festooned with cobwebs, and unused agricultural implements stood in the corners. The barns were not comfortable, they were not hygienic, but they were a shelter against the bitter March winds that blew across Flanders. And so Private Atkins piled on all the clothes he possessed, put his feet in his pack, lay back in the straw and slept like a god, just as his ancestors had done when they fought for Queen Anne in the same neighbourhood.

For about ten days the battalion remained billeted in farms. The time was spent in various forms of training, including the use of primitive jam tin bombs. There were lectures, tactical schemes, route marches and trench digging. This period gave all ranks a further breathing space before actually going under fire.

C

CHAPTER V

At last orders were received for the battalion to proceed to the trenches. This was really splendid; everybody was delighted because they wanted to know what it felt like to be under fire, and to see what real trenches looked like. They were thoroughly tired of digging trenches and filling them in again.

And so on March 26th, a bleak Friday afternoon, they marched down the road to Armentières full of curiosity, esprit de corps and the joy of spring.

Major L. V. Wykes was in command, Lt.-Col. W. A. Harrison having been granted a month's sick leave in England.

At Le Bizet, a suburb of Armentières, the battalion was quartered in a large empty factory. It was much overcrowded, and there was hardly room to pass when all the men were lying down at night. If the Germans had dropped a shell in it, the casualties would have been frightful, and it was within easy range of their heavy artillery; however, nobody seemed to bother; troops had been housed there before and nothing had happened, so why worry?

A company at a time went into the trenches at Le Bizet for instruction from the 1st King's Own and the 2nd Essex Regiment who were holding that part of the line.

It was quite pleasant going up the long duck-board communication trench just as it was getting dusk; there was nothing terrifying about it, and then suddenly before you realised it you were in the front line and you heard shots being fired intermittently, which rather reminded you of a shooting gallery.

The trenches were clean, tidy and well drained, and they consisted principally of sandbag barricades; they had fair dug-out accommodation, and were well supplied with coke and braziers which were needed as the nights were very cold. A good many officers and men of the garrison had been in France since the beginning of the war, and they told tales of the retreat from Mons, and of the fraternisation with the Germans in "No Man's Land" on Christmas Day.

Each company under instruction was actually in the trenches for twenty-four hours, and the men settled down to their work well; they showed great interest in their new surroundings, were desperately keen about learning their job, and in consequence the Regulars seemed to think well of them.

This was the first meeting with the Regulars, and really the friendliness shown by these veterans was most marked. They could not do too much to make the Territorials as comfortable as possible, and were at great pains to impart all the information they thought most useful, and generally instruct them in the art of trench warfare, and certainly their trenches set the battalion a high standard to live up to.

Yes, there was much to be learned, peering into the darkness on sentry duty, keeping still when Verey lights went up, and "standing to" an hour before dawn and dark. They saw men hit, bandaged and carried down the communication trench on stretchers. They were taught that steel loopholes were dangerous, that large periscopes were unhealthy, and that smoke was simply an invitation to the sniper, and they began to realise that trench warfare consisted much more of fatigues than fighting.

It was a quiet part of the line, but at the end of the tour of duty the casualties amounted to one killed and three wounded.

When not actually in the trenches the time was spent digging a second line of defence about a mile in rear. Here companies came under fire from "whizz-bangs," but no one was hit, though there were many narrow escapes, and quite a number of the noses of these small shells were collected as souvenirs and surreptitiously sent home as opportunity arose. The digging was done close to an old Flemish farm bearing the date 1702, a pleasant place in times of peace.

On March 31st the battalion left Le Bizet and marched back to its billets at Steenwerck. All ranks were thoroughly happy and felt just like schoolboys on the first day of the holidays (it is curious how coming out of the trenches always brought just that feeling) : besides they were gratified at last to have heard bullets fired in anger (whatever that may mean). They were soldiers now, they had something to write home about, and there was no possibility of the war finishing without a shot being fired by the 4th Leicesters. They were now ready to hold a piece of line of their own, and they did not have long to wait.

CHAPTER VI

On April 1st the brigadier informed the battalion that in a day or two it would move into the trenches, and there was no April fooling about this statement. For the next day (Good Friday) the orders were received for the battalion to move to rest billets at Dranoutre on the day following, and to proceed to take over the trenches occupied by the 1st Monmouths.

The battalion duly marched eight miles to Dranoutre via Bailleul, and was billeted in farms bearing such names as "Hyderabad," "Ava" and "Khandahar," quite pleasant places with the usual chilly stone-floored room for the officers, and the draughty, verminous, stale-strawed barns for the men. Everybody rather turned up their noses at these billets, but after the first tour in the trenches, these same places were being called "home."

Major T. T. Gresson, D.S.O., York and Lancaster Regiment, assumed command on this day (April 3rd). He was a Regular.

The same evening the company commanders and their seconds-in-command visited the trenches they were to take over on the morrow. They assembled at battalion headquarters, which was a small house opposite Dranoutre Church, and then walked up three miles of road to Lindenhoek, and then through fields to One Tree Farm, which was the battalion headquarters of the 1st Monmouths.

Not a glimmer of light from the farm; it was supposed that the Germans thought it deserted. No smoke was ever allowed to go up its chimney, and no one was to be seen in its vicinity by day. A wonderful contraption of blankets guarded its door so that no glimpse of light should show. Inside was a coke brazier, whose fumes almost choked every newcomer. Sleeping orderlies lay in a corner on a pile of blankets; tired-eye telephonists in earpieces sat at a table in front of pink message forms. The regimental sergeant-major was the presiding deity in this room and the trusty henchman in the next, where sat the colonel and the adjutant.

The colonel had a solemn look and a black moustache; he received the Leicestershire officers cordially, and they sat or stood around the tiny room, which was now crowded. There was much conferring between the two C.O.'s with promptings from the adjutants and interruptions from the seconds-in-command. Trench maps were produced, trench garrisons allotted and the reserves of ammunition and tools disclosed.

The officers, having received their instructions, left one by one with the necessary guides, who led them through the darkness to the trenches they were to occupy and, having inspected them, (with the exception of O.C. "A" Company (Captain B. F. Newill) who remained in the line), they wearily trudged back to their companies at Dranoutre, arriving there as Easter Day dawned.

In an inner room of a little house at Dranoutre at 7 and 8 a.m. the padre of the brigade (Rev. P. Ashby) celebrated Holy Communion. Many officers and men attended, and the little room was very full. For a great many this was their last Easter Communion, and they knew it ; the fact was patent, even to the least imaginative, but what did it matter, what did they care, for were they not bending the knee to One who also died in a good cause ? And the "comfortable words" seemed even more comfortable than before.

At 11 a.m. the battalion assembled in a bare field for Church Parade ; the dress was field service marching order, as the battalion might be required to move at any moment in an emergency and the billets were scattered. The battalion, pack on back, listened quietly to the service, mumbled the "Lord's Prayer," voluntarily pulled itself to attention for the "Creed" according to its custom, and sang lustily the hymn, doubtless carefully chosen for the occasion, "The fight is o'er, the battle won," knowing full well that they were going into something suspiciously like a battle that self-same evening.

The general situation on the Western Front at the time that the 4th Leicesters took over the trenches at Kemmel was this.

Neuve Chapelle, the first determined attempt in 1915 to break through the German lines, had ended in stalemate. A great many Regular officers and men, who were quite irreplaceable, had been killed in this battle and very little had been gained but a line or two of trenches and a lot of experience.

The only other British troops in France at this time, besides the Regulars, were Indian troops, various Territorial units attached to Regular divisions, the 1st Canadian Division, and the Territorial divisions which were coming over as soon as they were completely equipped.

The front line was held principally by Regular troops, but the Territorials were being trained in trench warfare as soon as they arrived.

The policy of the higher command was to construct one continuous line of trenches from the Belgians in the North to the French in the South, as at this period there were very many gaps in the line, and isolated posts which could only be relieved at night. A larger number of men were required to construct these works and to man them when constructed. Thus, in spite of the influx of Territorial divisions, the reserves behind the line were very meagre, because so many troops were needed in the trenches.

There was an adage, current at this period, which maintained that "the Germans held their front line with machine guns, the French with 75s, and the British with men." There was a very great deal of truth in this, and the fact of the matter was that the British were so hopelessly short of shells and machine guns that, if the line was to be held securely, there had to be a large garrison in the front line trenches which meant tremendous waste of human life.

This shortage of munitions was the direct outcome of the criminal parsimony and sloppy sentimentalism of the Liberal Government which had been in power since 1906 and whose leaders knew perfectly well that a European war was imminent. Lord Roberts had warned them unceasingly, even Robert Blatchford had tried to rouse them from their lethargy, but without effect. And now that war had come they were paying for their folly with the lives of their sons and the sons of the whole nation. The unpreparedness of the British Government for war in 1914 is one of the most hideous crimes that stains the pages of our history. It was like sending a gladiator into the arena with a tin sword.

At 8.30 p.m. on Easter Sunday, April 4th, the battalion assembled in column of route on the Dranoutre-Lindenhoek road and marched to One Tree Farm. It was quite dark when they arrived there except for the Verey lights which were going up intermittently all along the line in the distance. The silence was broken only by desultory rifle fire in the trenches, the rumble of limbered transport wagons, and every now and then by a spent bullet which pinged its way into the ground like a tired bumblebee.

The troops stood about for some time while officers received orders, rations and coke were issued and guides detailed. A corpse under a blanket was carried by on a stretcher; the men saw it, whispered to one another and were silent. They realised that they were waiting in the field adjoining the slaughter house.

The relief of the 1st Monmouths was completed that night, though with a good deal of difficulty. Through inexperience, instead of keeping on the dry ground, water-logged communication trenches were used in which men were up to their waists in mud, touch in some cases was lost, and men got into the wrong trenches, water carried up in dixies was nearly all spilled, bags of coke and rations were lost in the mud, and the weather was wet and dismal.

The trenches which the battalion took over were on the western slope of the Messines Ridge at a place called the Span-broekmolen, which once had been a mill, though very few traces of it remained. The Germans held the crest of the ridge and drained all their filth into our trenches which were halfway down. Our distance from the enemy varied from 30 to 100 yards. The so-called trenches were in reality sandbag barricades. They were in poor condition owing to the wet weather, there was not a decent dug-out in the front line, and in most trenches it was impossible to dig without at once coming to water or dead bodies.

The ground had been much fought over. A six-horse gun team complete in harness lay in one place; blue-coated, red-trousered Frenchmen were to be found in most ditches. There were many corpses of men of the 3rd Worcestershires and 1st Wiltshires lying about. They had attacked at very short notice on March 12th to prevent the Germans sending troops from that sector to Neuve Chapelle. The bombardment had been inaccurate, the wire was not cut and they had lost very heavily in consequence. And there they lay in "No Man's Land," their rifles with bayonets fixed beside them, and one of them, poor fellow, was found with his pipe filled in his pocket ready to smoke when the attack was over.

There were rows of stunted willows whose branches now drooped sadly, half cut through by bullets, and the birds sat in them and chirruped every morning at "stand to," for the war did not seem to bother them in the least.

This first tour of four days was from the point of view of discomfort one of the most trying experienced by the battalion. Mud was everywhere; in the food, in the tea, in the boots, in the eyes. Dug-outs were practically non-existent, men sat under waterproof sheets on the firing step, gulped down the rum ration, dozed and wished for day. Officers and telephonists were little better off; if they had a piece of corrugated iron and a couple of sandbags as a roof they were lucky. Efforts were made to drain, efforts were made to pump, but no pump was known to remain serviceable for more than an hour as very few men understood them.

One morning in F2 trench there was a sudden crash on the parapet; our gunners had dropped one short. A corporal was mortally wounded and died soon afterwards, another man's arm was practically blown off (he now plays a good game of golf with one arm) and a pencil was neatly taken from between the fingers of a third man who was writing a letter. The advantage of being a gunner is that you only get shot at by one side.

Getting the wounded away from the front line was very difficult as the enemy from their commanding position could see the ground behind our trenches, and the communication trenches leading to the supports were practically impassable, especially for stretchers. The stretcher bearers, who were mostly bandsmen, some well ripening in age, behaved magnificently, and passed all possible expectations. They worked like Trojans, and by tremendous effort got the wounded away.

At the end of four days the battalion was relieved by the 5th Lincolnshire Regiment. It was nearly dawn when the relief arrived, but it was misty. The Companies came out independently, reported at One Tree Farm, and proceeded to billets. It was a grey morning, it was a grey road, and the faces of the men were grey with fatigue. They could just put one foot in front of the other, and slowly and painfully they covered the three miles to Dranoutre. Colonel Gresson and the adjutant came riding by. "You must take your men home slowly, they are very tired," said the Colonel. But an hour-and-a-half later, passing near his billet in Dranoutre, the men sang as loud as they could in the hope of waking him up and showing him that they still had a kick left in them. When they reached billets they fell on the straw in their barns and straightway slept.

CHAPTER VII

"E.1 LEFT"

"E.1 This trench is in two parts, E.1 Right and E.1 Left, separated by 30x-40x old trench now being worked at. E.1 Right has 30 rifles, E.1 Left has 20, each should have an officer. Exposed position and liable to enfilade fire and sudden assault, but very important, has communication trench right up from S.P.1. Men should only be in this trench 24 hours and then relieved. Ground all round is insanitary."—Extract from Appendix "A" War Diary 4th Leicestershire Regiment.

It would take more than the pen of an Edgar Allan Poe to describe truthfully the gruesomeness, the noisome atmosphere and the unutterable filth of E.1 Left. The Regulars had called it "Hell's Kitchen," and there is probably no better or worse name for it.

It consisted of an isolated sandbag barricade near the Span-broekmolen. It was built on dead bodies of both French and British, which had been partially smothered with filth and chloride of lime ; it was about 15 yards in length and about 30 yards from the German lines and slightly below them. It had no shelter of any sort when the Leicesters arrived, though afterwards it was improved slightly and a dug-out built. It posted listening patrols of two men each to its right and left fronts and its occupants sent up flares most of the night.

No one got any sleep during the twenty-four hours of duty, or much food, as, directly there was any sign of cooking, the Germans, who had absolute superiority of fire, sniped the tops of the sandbags, so that dirt flew into the tea and into the food, and to put a head over the parapet in the daytime meant instant death with brains flying in all directions.

On a wet, dark, cold night a couple of officers (one of them Capt. B. F. Newill, O.C. "A" Coy.) in macintoshes and gum boots hurry over the intervening space between E.1 Right and E.1 Left slipping into pools of water on the way. In E.1 Left they find the sentries on duty very much on the alert, peering over the parapet into the darkness and crouching motionless when the flares go up. There, under a waterproof sheet, sits a very junior subaltern (Second-Lieut. A. C. Clarke) ; he has just visited the listening post ; everything is all right ; the only thing he wants is chloride of lime ; why hasn't it come up ? He requisitioned for it this morning, these dead Frenchmen smell so abominably. Yes, he will have a cigarette ; he has smoked most of his own or given them to the men ; everything is all right, though it is beastly wet; the ammunition is under a waterproof sheet; "but, for goodness sake, send up some chloride of lime; several of the men have been sick already; it's these dead Frenchmen."

This is the pitiful story of E.1 Left. A wretched little post "but very important." Held by the French who leave their dead unburied; then by the Regulars through the comfortless winter of 1914-1915, when twenty men splash into it on a dark night and eight of them stagger out of it when relieved forty-eight hours later. Now the Leicesters hold it with twenty-four hour reliefs; they work hard at it, they improve it, they build a dug-out and a traverse, they bury some of the putrifying bodies of the Frenchmen, others they smother in lime. They lose many good men shot through the head. Second-Lieut. K. Dalgliesh sups off toasted cheese, goes out to visit the listening patrol, gets a bullet in the arm, and carries an empty sleeve for the rest of his life.

So it goes on, and this grim trench takes its daily toll of life like some foul ogre. On some days it is hungrier than others, as on May 10th when five or six Germans of the 5th Bavarian Infantry bomb it, led by a tall six-foot-three-inch officer, reputed to be a defaulter and therefore detailed for the job. It is half-an-hour before midnight; everything is very quiet all round. The Germans do not appear to be firing at all, and officers and sentries are just beginning to wonder what is the reason of the unusual silence. When suddenly several loud explosions are heard from E.1 Left, accompanied by flashes. Everybody "stands to," the word comes on the telephone that E.1 Left has been taken by the enemy. Immediately from all directions lead is pumped into this miserable trench, flares go up all round, the German gunners put over salvoes. Colonel Gresson hurriedly leaves the funeral of Second-Lieut. A. C. Clarke at One Tree Farm, and quickly makes arrangements for a general engagement. Capt. T. P. Fielding-Johnson organises a counter attack from E.6 trench, and it is led by Second-Lieut. C. P. Peake, who has only joined the battalion from England the previous day and is in the trenches for the first time. It is not a pleasant job struggling up the slope with fixed bayonets in the light of Verey flares, and not knowing when a burst of enemy fire may come from E.1 Left. However, the trench is reached without opposition, and Captain H. Haylock, its commander, is found to be dying by the side of a dead German officer and Sergeant Jacques, who is also dead. The Germans had thrown about seven bombs, two of which exploded in the trench, and had then retired leaving their officer behind.

The trench is regarrisoned and life in it continues to be comfortless and death frequent.

There is a sequel, however. A certain private soldier, who

was in E.1 Left at the time of the raid, is missing. What has happened to him? Nobody knows. But have the Germans "bumped out of him" any information regarding the mining going on behind E.1 Left? The mining sergeant of the Monmouths, who are working there, thinks they have, as he can now hear the Germans mining and coming nearer and nearer. On May 20th E.1 Left is blown sky high. From Dranoutre it looks like a dirty yellow cloud hanging in the air. The 5th Lincolns are occupying it. Lieut. Dyson is buried in the telephone dug-out for four hours, but is got out alive. Lieut. Gosling, a fine young R.E. officer, dashes straight across from E.1 Right in broad daylight to give assistance and is killed. The work of digging out the survivors goes on furiously under fire. Major Adlercron, the brigade major, comes up and helps to superintend the operations. A new E.1 Left rises on the ruins of the old; and two stone-dead Lincolns, who have been hanging in the parapet for three days, are carried away with the first streaks of dawn of Whit-Sunday by the Leicesters who have just relieved.

And so it goes on. Men come jauntily and are carried away haltingly and by stealth. The birds sing in the shot-riddled willows, and the rats become super-rats. This little plot of ground not so far from the mill, which for years was just a pleasant little piece of pasture land, growing a little grass for a few sheep, has now gained notoriety and has been dubbed by the great warriors "but very important," and by the lesser warriors "that bloody 'ole E.1 Left."

Thank God, it has now lost its ill-starred importance, and all is as it used to be, save that the grass grows a deeper green.

CHAPTER VIII

THE COMING OF MARTIN

FROM April 3rd to May 21st the battalion stayed at Dranoutre, then it moved to bivouac on Kemmel Hill where it remained until June 22nd. During this time it did duty in the trenches with unceasing regularity four days in and four days out, being relieved by the 5th Lincolns.

Most of the trenches were less unpleasant than E.1 Left, and by dint of hard work and with the advent of fine weather they became well drained and paved with duck-boards. The parapets were made bullet-proof, and the communication trenches improved beyond recognition, so that access to the front line was easy and safe.

In fact, life was not too bad; a little mining, a little shelling, and the New Army battalions coming in for instruction, which gave more men for fatigues, though it crowded the dug-out accommodation.

The battalion is a happy battalion, everything goes smoothly, everybody does his best and seems to get a little credit for it. However is this? What is the reason? The answer is simple :— "Martin has come."

Only those who were serving with the battalion at that time will realise just how much those three words meant. On May 22nd Major R. E. Martin rode up to battalion headquarters at the bivouac on Kemmel Hill to take over command of the 4th Leicestershires vacated by Lieut.-Col. T. T. Gresson owing to ill-health, and the golden age of the 4th Leicestershire Regiment began.

Major R. E. Martin came from the 5th Leicestershire Regiment of which he had been second-in-command : they did not want to lose him and he was of two minds about leaving them, until Colonel Jones of the 5th told him that promotion must never be refused and that settled it. He was a big man, but a thin man; he never looked very well and probably never felt very well; he wore spectacles and a big fair moustache; he spoke highbrow English in a high-pitched voice; he called a dead cow a "vociferous heifer," and a tin mug a "drinking receptacle"; but he knew how to build dug-outs; he understood the bonding of sandbags, he procured timber from unlikely places and corrugated iron and tarred felt as if by sleight of hand. He thought of everything and everybody except possibly himself; he never appeared to be put out; he seldom "straffed"; but he expected much and his expectations were generally realised. He

LIEUTENANT-COLONEL R. E. MARTIN, C.M.G., T.D., D.L.

was the best all-round soldier in the battalion, and the battalion knew it and only got annoyed with him when he exposed himself to danger unnecessarily, which was one of his habits. He rode on the snaffle and had little use for the spur.

The bivouac on Kemmel Hill was pleasant, the nights were warm, the nightingales sang, the country round was a beautiful rich, dark green, and dotted about the landscape were homely red-tiled farm houses. It was enjoyable to jog into Bailleul on the company horse for a bath at the asylum and then go to tea at the "Faucon" or at "Tina's."

Everybody knew Tina ; she was a very engaging young lady and she kept a tea-shop with her mother and did a roaring trade. She talked to everybody, she joked with the gay ones, she took the shy ones into the garden and showed them snapshots of herself. She collected cap badges and stuck them in large sheets of cardboard ; she had one of almost every regiment and a chaplain's into the bargain. One sometimes wonders what has happened to her, whether she was still there when the Germans advanced in 1918, and whether she has now settled down peacefully in the district as a godly matron. There were rumours that she was removed from Bailleul because she knew too much of the military situation from the gossip of the officers she met ; there was a tale that she was shot as a spy. Who knows ? But one thing is certain ; she did much for the Brighter Bailleul movement in 1915.

May passed, and a warm June came. Life in the trenches was much more comfortable, the casualties were less and the better dug-outs had wire and sand-bag beds. Leave started, beginning with the most wonderful sight in the world, the white cliffs of Dover seen from the leave boat, and ending five days later with that twentieth-century Gethsemane—Victoria Station.

Captain R. S. Dyer-Bennet, the adjutant, was wounded while roaming about No Man's Land at night without notifying the sentries in the vicinity. He had a New Army adjutant with him and they were lucky to escape with their lives as our sentries were taking no risks.

On June 7th Second-Lieut. F. M. Waite was killed in E.1 Left by a bullet, and on June 10th Lieut. H. C. Brice died of wounds caused by the premature bursting of a rifle grenade which he was instructing the Lincolns how to use. They were both first-class officers and the best fellows in the world, and the heart of the battalion was heavy with grief.

One hot afternoon Major-General Milne (now Field-Marshal Lord Milne, late Chief of the Imperial General Staff,) came quietly through the trenches. On being shown a shell hole made that morning close to the officers' dug-out by a German 13-inch he laughed and asked the company commander what he had done to deserve it, thus putting him at his ease at once. He asked a lot of questions about conditions in the trenches, called the German multi-coloured parapet a work of art, said that they were a very clever people and would take a lot of beating, and passed on smiling urbanely—a veritable "Uncle George."

Then came rumours of "Ypres." Everybody knew what a visit there meant. Shelling by day and night, gas attacks, mines, bombing and all kinds of bloodiness. Had they not watched Ypres burning in the distance? Had they not sniffed the gas from afar, and seen the casualty lists? They had, but they did not mind; they were ready to go anywhere. And on the night of the 18th of June, the hundredth anniversary of Waterloo, the 4th Leicesters swung out of the trenches that they had made the best in the whole line and left the Messines Ridge for ever.

COMPANY SERGEANT-MAJOR HUNT AND
SERGEANT BURDETT IN YPRES
TRENCHES, 1915.

CORPORAL KENT WITH A PERISCOPIC
RIFLE, YPRES, 1915.

TRENCH 47, YPRES, 1915.

CHAPTER IX

YPRES

"WIPERS" has an immortal place in the annals of the British Army around which legends will be woven and tales told until the end of time, when the present town will be a wilderness once more and the Menin Gate a crumbling relic of a past belligerent age.

But Ypres has a personality of its own and it impresses in varying degree everyone who passes that way. Perhaps it is the atmosphere created by the thousands of gallant men who fought and died there, perhaps it is the legacy of more ancient times, probably it is both. But the Spirit of the place is felt to-day by all who stand before the Menin Gate and gaze on the Latin inscription to the British dead, "Pro Rege, Pro Patria." And during the war the same spirit was felt by every British soldier who passed through the Menin Gate and read the unseen writing on the ramparts, "See Wipers and die."

On the 22nd of June the battalion left Dranoutre and marched through the warm summer night to Ouderdom, a hamlet a few miles from Ypres, where by midnight it was bivouaced in an open field. There it remained for a week, resting, route marching, bayonet fighting. It was flooded out by the torrential rain of a heavy thunderstorm, but it dried itself and was as cheerful as ever.

It was a pleasant bivouac. There was a farmhouse with its usual supplies of café au lait; there was a homely-looking windmill; there were one or two cows and a very young bull in a field; there was also "Les Trois Amis," an estaminet, where bock was supplied in a little back garden where one sat on a rickety chair by a tin-topped table and the daughter of the house (a rather plain girl) wearing a black dress and black cotton stockings came to and fro with the glasses.

It was warm summer weather and for a week it was not a bad war, even though shells dropped on our horse lines a hundred yards in rear, which caused the woman at the farmhouse to go first into tears, then into hysterics and finally into the cellar.

A new draft, ninety-one strong, arrived and were duly inspected by the brigadier and the divisional commander who regaled them with the usual time-honoured questions such as, "How old are you?" "What do you do in civilian life?" and "Do your new boots fit all right?" This draft included Sergeant Stevenson, who had been at Bishops Stortford with the battalion and used to lead the band which played at all the officers' dances and whose

31

rendering of the waltzes, "Venus on Earth" and "Nights of Gladness," was particularly efficient. He was a cheery, red-faced fellow and a general favourite. He made but one trip to the trenches ; a shell burst over his dug-out and he was found to be dead, but without a scratch.

Orders came for the officers to visit the sector to be taken over by the battalion, and Major J. A. Potter, who was temporarily in command, set off with the O.'s C. companies for Sanctuary Wood.

This meant mounting the company horse at three o'clock in the afternoon and riding along a wagon track for two or three miles to Kruisstraat. What a track it was ; pleasant enough to gallop along as it was soft to the horse's feet, but when the battalion marched on it everybody was covered with dust from head to foot. All sorts and conditions of soldiery passed along it ; mounted staff officers with orderlies riding behind at a respectful distance ; galloping Belgian interpreters hanging on by their spurs ; limbered wagons with highly burnished hubs, obviously belonging to some Regular unit with a proper appreciation of spit and polish ; R.E. with mules bearing telephone equipment ; an occasional Sepoy with thin legs and inscrutable countenance ; an occasional section of field guns ; an occasional platoon. In fact, anything and anybody who had any bearing on the war passed that way during the day, easily, jauntily, two or three together, not much to do and all day to do it in.

It was at night that the track became really imposing, an artery up which flowed the blood for the Salient. Every evening infantry battalions could be seen "going up" complete, swelled with recent drafts. Every evening miles of limbered wagons bumped and clanked bearing rations, water, S.A.A., R.E. stores and the post. Sometimes the weather was wet and the rain streamed off the waterproof sheets which covered the men's shoulders. Sometimes the weather was hot and dry and the sweat poured off their foreheads. Sometimes the air was charged with thunder, always with blasphemy. Sometimes there was a block in the narrow street of Kruisstraat. Sometimes the transport was shelled during the block ; then there were casualties, then mules broke loose in the dark, and a pleasant summer evening became the "hell of a night." But nevertheless the rations were delivered and the reliefs completed.

Then in the early mornings the transport could be seen coming back at the trot, everybody happy, even the mules ; and battalions "coming out" dog tired, dirty, dusty, mostly lousy, sometimes sadly depleted, strange dark figures of men and horses silhouetted against the first grey streaks of dawn, with the mouth organs in full song.

Such was the track from Ouderdom to Kruisstraat.

On the occasion in question the officers dismounted at Kruis-straat, left the horses, and now the way to Sanctuary Wood is by bridge 14, two by two as the path is pock-marked with shell holes, for the Boches who observe from the top of Hill 60 snipe with whizz-bangs. Then comes Zillebeke Village and Zillebeke Church with the windows stuffed with very obvious sandbags, the work of some genius, and it draws a lot of shell fire. Then the path runs by a hedge, past a dead horse and then by a canvas screen pitted with bullet holes ; next comes a thick leafy wood. This is Maple Copse ; presumably the Canadians, whose badge is a maple leaf, have been here. There is half a battalion of Regulars in it now busy playing "house." And an aeroplane sentry is on duty who blows a whistle every time he sees an aeroplane, and then everybody keeps still until someone shouts "One of ours" or the enemy plane disappears.

Finally Sanctuary Wood. What a delightful place it is, all green and bosky. Everything is quiet except for a little firing from the trenches on its eastern edge. Very nasty, bloody trenches those, very apt to get direct hits from high explosive shells. The Regulars have kept very quiet here for the last few weeks ; they have sat on their hunkers and played "house," and the Boches have left them alone.

But now the 46th Division have arrived. They have a reputation for trench making. The piece of line they have left at Kemmel is the model of the whole Front. They must keep up their reputation. They must construct palatial headquarters dug-outs, strengthen strong points and improve trenches. Working parties are busy by day. Thousands of sandbags are filled, all sorts of material are brought up. And the wily old Boche sees it all, or at any rate some of it, and over come the Krumps and down go the palatial dug-outs, and up go the occupants. And the evening "hate" becomes angrier, and the ambulances go away fuller and the leaves, yes, and the branches fall from the trees in June, and the wood becomes less green and less bosky, in fact, it is becoming decidedly unhealthy.

At 7 p.m. on June 29th the battalion paraded at Ouderdom to proceed to Sanctuary Wood to relieve the 5th Sherwood Foresters. By 1.30 a.m. the relief was complete.

The weather was gloriously hot and life in the wood was pleasant except for the shelling. It was very obvious to everyone that Kemmel was a health resort compared to Ypres. There were shells that rumbled through the air like flying tramcars, and to listen to their approach gave one a very disconcerting feeling in the pit of the stomach, because as they rumbled nearer and nearer one was never quite sure whether they were going to rumble on (probably into Ypres) or whether the dug-out in which one happened to be shivering was going to metaphorically

D

"back a winner," in which case there would be another dirty job for the gallant but splay-footed Corporal Wright and the stretcher bearers.

The front line was heavily "Krumped" during the tour, and for fifteen minutes one evening the wood was absolutely deluged with shrapnel. The battalion was lucky to have only five killed and twelve wounded in the six days. They had worked hard and had got a good deal done when they were relieved by the 6th South Staffords on the night of July 5th. The companies marched back independently to Ouderdom covering the eight miles by 5 a.m. the next day. They were very dusty and weary when they arrived, but the company quartermaster-sergeants (those much maligned individuals) saw that they got plenty of breakfast, issued the blankets and then everybody slept.

It was a wonderful summer morning ; the sun shone, the air was fresh, there was not a cloud in the sky. It felt very good to be alive and be back again by the quiet peaceful-looking old windmill, with the prospect of six days' rest, very good to be out of the wood, altogether too much stuff flying about up there. And the M.O. (MacAlister Hewlings) who with a fatherly eye has watched the battalion march in says :—"Here, have a whisky: it will do you good." And evidently it does do you good, for you slip into your valise and drop off to sleep without a care in the world and dream of "Ouderdom for the Holidays. Recommended by the Medical Profession. Fireworks every evening on the Front."

CHAPTER X

"SIX DAYS SHALT THOU REST"

THE phrase "six days' rest" was really a snare and a delusion. In the imagination one looked forward to sleep unlimited, parcels from home galore; letters from at least half-a-dozen armfuls of delicious womanhood alluding affectionately to the joys of past and future "leaves." One had visions of binges in Bailleul, razzles in Reninghelst, and perchance passion in Poperinghe. But in reality "six days' rest" was an entirely different affair. Certainly it began with parcels and sleep, followed by baths and clean clothes, but after that it was sadly tarnished by "The C.O. will inspect," "The battalion will parade," or "A Working Party will be furnished," which meant that companies had to pull themselves together and remember that they were soldiers once more and not semitroglodytes living in trenches and dug-outs. And that as soldiers they had to stand smartly to "atten-tion," to "fix bayonets," to keep the thumb in line with the seam of the trousers, and the feet at an angle of forty-five degrees. And, after the morning had been energetically spent in drill and bayonet fighting, they would be gratified to hear that there would be a route march in the afternoon.

On one of these days of rest, July 11th, the battalion paraded at 5 a.m. 600 strong for digging fatigue, marched to the White Chateau at Kruisstraat, and dug for six hours on the support line which was being constructed just in front of Ypres.

The C.R.E. was very pleased with the amount of work done, which was not surprising, because when the 4th Leicesters were given a job of work they really got down to it; the company commanders saw to that. There was no sitting about smoking cigarettes, no leaning on shovels in soulful admiration of the landscape, no furtive falling out to suck water-bottles. The sleeves were rolled up, the tools issued, the task allotted; and then the picks and shovels got to work and a meadow became a strong point almost as if by a magician's wand.

Everybody worked, and though it was the job of the officers and N.C.O.'s to superintend, yet they all lent a hand in the digging and enjoyed doing it. There was plenty of grousing, plenty of profanity, plenty of perspiration, but there was a lot of work. No wonder the C.R.E. smiled.

There was a certain corporal, however, who had an abhorrence of disturbing the soil and turning over the sods himself, though he simply loved seeing his section do it and gave them any amount of verbal encouragement. Being a fat and jolly humorist

35

and the star turn at all smoking concerts, he regaled those digging with snappy incidents from his past life, reeled off yards of music hall patter and related the most intriguing stories, always prefacing his remarks with "Now, 'ave you 'eard this one?"   Of course he kept them in fits of laughter, but he kept them at work, and if an officer came his way he busied himself by giving a dissertation to some perspiring private on the correct use of the pick or shovel. His name was ——. Ah, well, live and let.

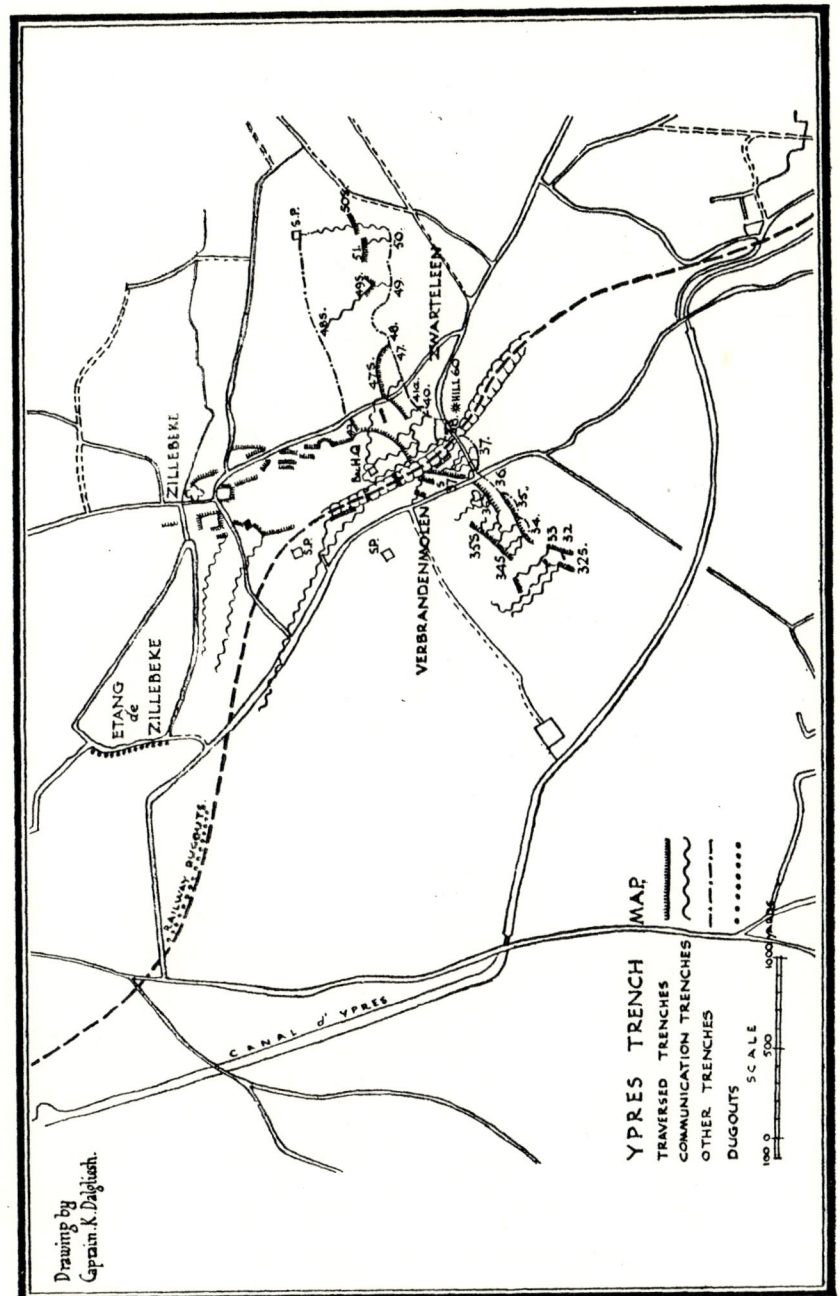

YPRES TRENCH MAP.

TRAVERSED TRENCHES
COMMUNICATION TRENCHES
OTHER TRENCHES
DUGOUTS

SCALE

Drawing by
Captain. K. Dalgliesh.

CHAPTER XI

HILL 60

On the evening of July 13th the battalion left its bivouac at Ouderdom, and took over from the 1st Dorsets the dug-outs in the embankment of the Ypres-Commines Railway near Zillebeke Lake, and also some strong points in the vicinity.

In peace time Zillebeke must have been a pleasant place. There was a lake on which, doubtless, rowing boats plied, and on fine Sunday afternoons it was probably thronged with holiday-makers. It was an entirely different place now. In the embankment of the lake there were dug-outs facing away from the lake, and opposite them in the side of the railway embankment were the dug-outs which the Leicesters now occupied. They were by no means safe and hardly shrapnel-proof, they let in the rain, and a few well-directed "Krumps" would soon have destroyed them and their occupants. However, they gave some shelter from the elements and a certain feeling of security. The Germans had never paid them more attention than a few "whizz-bangs" and an occasional "Krump," so everyone made themselves comfortable and hoped for the best.

The supports for the front line held these dug-outs, and were employed at night on carrying and digging fatigues, and had orders to be seen as little as possible. So the daytime was spent in idleness, a lot of sleep, a good deal of cards and a little fishing with bent pins in the pond.

In the space between the lake and the railway dug-outs was a road up which the transport rumbled at night, a line of poplars which were gradually becoming more war-worn and a little cemetery which was steadily getting bigger. In the distance stood Ypres and the battered Cloth Hall daily getting more of a ruin, and just outside Ypres the red brick Ecole de Bienfaisance, which the Germans shelled industriously daily raising dust clouds of couleur de rose.

Owing to the rising ground eastward the railway embankment soon ended, and the railway ran along the level for a little way, then into a cutting and finally into the German lines. On the North of this cutting was Hill 60, so called from the ring contour marking it on the large scale maps. It was in reality an artificial mound made from the earth excavated in making the cutting. Anyone who goes to Hill 60 now and stands by the Memorial on its crest will realise what it meant to the Germans. It gave them a wonderful view of the whole Salient, and enabled them to see any movement of troops ; but there was also a magnificent view eastwards right back to Commines, and, if the British could have held the crest, it would have been a tremendous advantage to them, and made life for those in the Salient much less precarious.

Hill 60, therefore, was of very considerable military importance. The British had taken it on April 17th, but they had been unable to hold it. There had been heavy fighting on it, and also one of the German gas attacks had been launched there with considerable success; the gas had hung about the cutting and there had been many casualties.

So already this was historic ground and the atmosphere was charged with uncertainty and occasional "whizz-bangs," and one felt that anything might happen at any time. This was the fighting part of the Front, though not very obviously, for it seemed just an ordinary railway cutting with the metals intact, no one was in sight except an orderly or two peeping out of the headquarters dug-out in the cutting. Hill 60 looked just a bare barren waste; and south of the railway there was a scarred-looking wood on the horizon and a wrecked red brick building, which was once the Verbranden Molen. It was advisable, however, to step warily, for the all-seeing Boche on the high ground had ordained that where two or three were gathered together there should be a "whizz-bang" in the midst of them.

From July 13th to the 19th the battalion remained comfortably in the railway dug-outs basking in the sunshine and complacently watching Ypres being shelled during the day and uncomplainingly carrying out fatigues by night. So far so good.

On the 18th, however, there was a tragedy. Lieut. F. N. Tarr was killed. You had to know Frank Tarr and to be in the battalion to realise what that meant; no words can ever explain.

He was killed by a splinter from a "Krump" whilst he was visiting the Zillebeke Lake dug-outs. The Boche was industriously shelling a field cooker which stood under a hedge close by, and Tarr put his head out of a dug-out to tell some men to keep under cover when a splinter hit him in the face. If it had been any other part of his body it would have caused only the slightest of wounds, a mere scratch, but that only made it more tragic. This happened in the afternoon.

That night, surrounded by his friends, he was buried not very far from where he had fallen, and the Brigade Chaplain (Rev. Paul Ashby) read the burial service. It was a sad night for everybody, for Frank Tarr was the most attractive personality in the battalion, young, good-looking, full of charm, with an eye that always had a twinkle in it, a born leader, yet the kindest person possible, a Rugger international, the idol of the machine-gun section, which he commanded before he became adjutant.

Everybody was heart-broken, for everybody would miss him; they would not look upon his like again.

And so, as the darkness fell, they buried him by stealth, with silent salutes and stifled tears. And the transport officer, who had played David to his Jonathan, caused a large white cross of wood to be made, a larger cross than any which stood around, that all who passed might see and remember a great three-quarter and a greater gentleman.

JUNCTION OF TRENCHES 47-48,
YPRES, 1915.

TRENCH 48, YPRES, 1915.

TRENCH 47, YPRES, 1915. *Left to right*, PRIVATE FOULKES, CORPORAL KENT,
SERGEANT BURDETT, SERGEANT GIBBONS.

CHAPTER XII

BLASTED MINES

NOTHING "puts the wind up" Private Atkins, T., so much as mines. He positively hates them, whether ours or the enemy's. If he hears rumours of mining or strange sounds underneath his trench he becomes fidgety and morose. He also takes umbrage if the R.E. arrive and begin tunnelling anywhere in his neighbourhood. He knows mining means counter-mining, and in his opinion the place becomes unhealthy and he decides it is getting on his nerves and vaguely wonders if it is worth while showing the M.O. his hammer toe, which he has borne so manfully for years, in the hope that he may be ordered a slight respite behind the lines in some salubrious spot well removed from ammonal and T.N.T. where his toe may have rest. The M.O. is all sympathy; he has a miraculous cure for hammer toes. He hands him a number nine and sees him swallow it.

Hill 60 and its vicinity was unmistakedly a "mining district," and the 4th Leicesters went right into the middle of it when on the night of July 19th they took over trenches 47, 48 and 49, just North of Hill 60. Trench 50 on their left was held by the 5th Leicestershires.

At 6.55 p.m. and 7.1 p.m. precisely on July 23rd the British exploded two mines under the German parapet opposite trench 50. A good many Boches went sky high and a good many were buried, but their comrades most courageously exposed themselves going to the rescue, while our guns deluged them with shrapnel for fifteen minutes, and we regaled them with rifle and machine-gun fire from the front line. This seemed satisfactory enough. "Nothing like knocking it out of the old Boche."

However, the soldiers of Kaiser Wilhelm II were not men to be trifled with; their motto was "One good mine deserves another," and so at 9.35 p.m. the same evening the Germans exploded a mine just short of trench 50, held by the 5th battalion. And in spite of the official communique, which stated that there were no casualties, about forty of the 5th were killed or wounded ; in fact, practically the whole garrison of the trench were put out of action.

"D" Company of the 4th Leicesters, who were holding 49 trench on the right of 50, immediately sent in bombers to hold what remained of trench 50. They also helped in digging out the buried men and putting the position in a state of defence once more.

After the explosion, trench 50 was just one-half acre of agony. Men were literally buried in heaps, one on the top of another, all mixed up with sandbags, beams of dug-outs, corrugated iron, machine-guns, rum jars and ammunition boxes. Arms and legs protruded from the debris, and cries and groans came from crumpled and broken heaps of humanity ejaculating "Oh, Jesus" and "For Christ's sake, get me out," half in imprecation, half in prayer. The 4th and 5th worked furiously to unearth the buried men. It was not an easy job because of the darkness and the difficulty of removing beams and debris from the top of men lest they should fall on others underneath. Shells were passing overhead, and our men on each side of trench 50 fired "rapid." The M.O. of the 5th (M. H. Barton) worked like a Trojan getting the wounded out, patching them up and sending them away, and by daylight the line was re-established and in a state of defence. Now the problem was what to do with the crater which was just short of what was left of the original front line parapet. It was decided to fortify it the following night.

So with the help of a combined fatigue party of R.E. and 4th and 5th Leicesters the work was begun on the night of the 24th. It consisted of filling sandbags and passing them over to the side of the crater nearest the enemy. Everybody put their heart and soul into the job ; sandbags were filled at a furious rate both in the trench and the crater. The ones from the trench had to be passed over the parapet, and as the moon was very bright (it generally was when any work had to be done in No Man's Land) the Boche saw signs of movement. And while Colonel Martin and Major Potter and thirty-five or forty men were working like blacks in the crater, the enemy threw a trench mortar bomb from a catapult which fell in the crater, killing one and wounding twenty-one men. This stopped work while the wounded were evacuated ; it was then carried on again until instructions were received from brigade to suspend work for half-an-hour to see if any more bombs were thrown. Two more were thrown, but they fell outside the crater, causing no casualties. By that time it was too light to resume work in the crater, but the job was completed the following night.

Colonel Martin was largely responsible for the arrangements for the fortification of the crater, which was a difficult and dangerous piece of work. Major Potter led the working parties and displayed great courage and coolness when the trench mortar bomb exploded in the crater, and was instrumental in getting the wounded safely away, and his personal example was of the greatest value in steadying the men. The moon shone serenely, but it was a very dirty night. And the men disliked mining even more than before.

CHAPTER XIII

A D'ARTAGNAN IN MINIATURE

AND so July passed and August came and went with its bombardments, its "Krumps" and "whizz-bangs," its working parties, its morning and evening "stand to's", its coveted "spots of leave."

The men were getting tired and war-worn, life and death in the Salient was a wearing business, many went to the field ambulance, and new officers arrived replacing casualties.

Men came staggering down the trenches on fatigues looking tired with grey faces, but they still carried on. There was a man who was sent to the M.O. and was reputed to have slept for forty-eight hours on end before the M.O. sent him back to the line.

The nights were getting colder; the rum ration was again issued. What rum it was, thirty per cent. over proof, and what a difference it made on a cold wet morning after a night spent in working and watching! One spoonful, how it warmed the feet, how it took the place of a blanket, and what sleep it brought, and that contented feeling which made Private Atkins sit happily on the firing step softly crooning himself to sleep with this refrain :—

> If the sergeants pinch the rum, never mind,
> If the sergeants pinch the rum, never mind,
>   They're entitled to a tot,
>   But they pinch the bloody lot,
>   If the sergeants pinch the rum, never mind.

The following incident shows the atmosphere which permeated the battalion :—

One night near the Verbranden Molen a man was hit belonging to a fatigue party carrying timber for mining; he was sent to a medical aid post nearby, and when the fatigue was over the officer in charge sent on the party and called to see how the man was. As it was not safe to walk about alone he selected a youngster out of the party to accompany him. This boy was a stocky little fellow who spent most of his time hanging over the parapet when his section commander was not looking; he was one of the rapid fire artists and the word fear was not in his vocabulary.

While the two were walking back to the railway dug-outs the officer for some reason or other asked the boy his age.

"Official or unofficial, sir," came the prompt reply.

"Unofficial, of course," said the officer.

"Well, sir, you promise you won't get me into trouble if I tell you ?"

"Not likely, and you need not think that I shall have you sent home if you are under age."

"I'm just sixteen," hissed the happy young warrior through his teeth. He always tried to look as bellicose as possible, and longed for the day when he would be able to grow a moustache like his company sergeant-major.

"Why did you join up so young ?" enquired the officer.

"Because all the other boys in our street were joining, and I wasn't going to be left behind."

Just sixteen and already under fire for six months !

The sequel happened a few days later.

The boy went down to the dressing station one morning with a stretcher party carrying a wounded N.C.O. On the way back through Armagh Wood they were caught by some shrapnel, and the boy was mortally wounded. In his agony he cried and called for his mother, and shortly afterwards he died.

He was a typical example of that comparatively rare species, "the born fighting man," a d'Artagnan in miniature. He enjoyed danger, he laughed at hardship, he loved fighting. Only a year or two previously he was playing at soldiers and Red Indians, but now here was the real thing all free, gratis and for nothing, and wasn't it fun ! Real rifles and bayonets, real bombs and, alas, real shrapnel.

And so passed as gallant a youngster as ever donned His Majesty's uniform ; doubtless Saint Michael has found a place for him in his host.

CHAPTER XIV

"BLESSED ARE THE MIRTHMAKERS"

In "B" Company there was a private soldier called Joe ——, who had a face that would have been the envy of George Robey or Mark Sheridan. He had beady little eyes, a long straight rubicund nose, and a tooth-brush moustache, which bristled over his comical mouth like a chevaux de frise guarding the entrance to the "Great Quart Way." For Joe was a thirsty soul.

He had been a Regular soldier, and had a good deal of rough and tumble fighting and a lot of serious drinking in most quarters of the globe. He was an accomplished barrack room lawyer with a thorough knowledge of King's Regulations ; and he could quote Shakespeare by the yard. He had an irritating habit of asking the subaltern of the day awkward questions when that officer visited the guardroom where Joe was confined every now and then.

But he had a wonderful sense of humour and seldom opened his mouth without emitting a witticism. He had a fund of all sorts of stories for all sorts of audiences, and he kept the men around him in fits of laughter when he related his adventures with sergeant-majors, major-generals and Indian princes. He was a born comedian and everybody in the battalion knew him.

Out of the trenches he gave his company commander considerable anxiety, as he was generally the victim of his insatiable thirst, and he was a great believer in celebrating superabundantly the last day in rest billets, with the result that he often marched up to the line with anything but a steady tread.

But once in the trenches he was the soul of industry and activity. He was as good or better than a sergeant, and could do any job and do it well. "Give me three men, sir, and I'll build the dug-out," he would say. And then under Joe's martial eye the best dug-out in the trench was erected, and the three men mopped great drops of sweat from their brows.

Early on the 30th of July the Germans, with the help of liquid fire, took some trenches at Hooge from the 14th Division, who were on the left of the 46th.

The 4th Leicesters were occupying Zillebeke Lake dug-outs, and about midnight on the 30th/31st they were suddenly ordered to "Stand to" as the Germans were attacking again. And "B" Company was ordered to hold itself in readiness to reinforce the line at Hooge.

It was a hot summer night and the men were standing about in "fighting order" ready to move. From Hooge came sounds of heavy bombardment, intense rifle and machine-gun fire, and the explosion of trench mortars and bombs. The woods were lit up by Verey lights and the red glare of liquid fire. Hooge looked a veritable inferno, and at any moment "B" Company might be ordered into this maelstrom of frightfulness.

As a natural result "B" Company was pensive, wondering what it would be like with the same uncomfortable expectancy one feels in a dentist's waiting room. At this moment Joe took the situation in hand.

"We're going over the top to-night, boys," he grinned. "Give your names to me all those wanting German 'elmets, German buttons and German bay'nits. I'll see you get 'em ; just give your names to me and say what you want ; any kind of souvenir you fancy," and so on and so forth ad lib. Joe's beady eyes twinkled, his eyebrows arched, his mouth assumed all manner of ribald contortions. Joe had never been more amusing. "B" Company rocked with mirth. The dentist's waiting room became the gallery of a music hall. The low comedian had arrived ; his salary was not a pound a week, but if ever a man earned a thousand a minute Joe did then.

At last the firing died down and the men went into the dug-outs, threw themselves down and slept.

Three months later Joe, a true son of Mars, lay dead on the field of honour surrounded by the men of "B" Company whom he had so often kept happy and amused.

Morale is everything, and Joe knew it.

CHAPTER XV

LICE, SUNSETS AND SHELLS

ON August 10th the battalion came out of the line and went back to rest at Ouderdom huts. It had been a long tour of duty, twenty eight days, and the battalion besides being very tired was very lousy. The "Chat," as the species of louse in question was called, was no respecter of persons. He paid his respects to the colonel; visited the adjutant; called on the company commanders; became attached to the platoon sergeants for rations, but not discipline; and fraternised only too freely with the rank and file. In some dug-outs men itched as soon as they sat down and as bathing facilities were entirely absent in the trenches they had to be content to scratch. During the hot afternoons men could be seen solemnly sitting on the firing step stripped to the waist with their shirts on their knees, at which they made fierce and sudden dives with their fingers, and on being asked what they were doing they invariably answered in the same four words: "Having a chat up." The origin of this expression and for how many centuries it has been current in His Majesty's Forces appears to be unknown.

The casualties during the twenty-eight days among the officers were Lieut. F. N. Tarr killed and Lieuts. Dunn and Nugee wounded. Of the other ranks there were 4 killed, 59 wounded, 31 sent to field ambulance, 25 war-worn sent to the base, who were replaced by a draft of 25.

This gives a fair idea of the wastage in the Salient during the ordinary course of trench warfare. For though there was heavy fighting at Hooge on July 19th and 22nd when the British attacked and on July 30th and 31st when the Germans retaliated with liquid fire attacks, and again on August 9th when the 6th Division successfully attacked, yet the 4th Leicesters had not been engaged in any actual attack or open fighting. Their losses were caused principally by shell fire, trench mortar bombs, commonly known as "sausages," and by snipers' bullets. The men who went to the field ambulance were generally suffering from trench fever, which usually consisted of diarrhoea and a temperature, and was largely caused by insanitary conditions and fatigue.

Things got pretty lively during the last week of the tour. The enemy trenches were shelled regularly every morning in the small hours, so that when the final bombardment took place on August 9th the Germans thought that it was the usual morning "hate" and were completely taken by surprise when the 6th

Division attacked at Hooge in one of the best-managed surprise engagements of the war.

It was very pleasant to hear our shells go screaming into the German lines just at the time when the rum was being issued. One smacked one's lips and murmured gleefully, "That's giving them hell," knowing full well that some time during the day, probably in the afternoon, the Boches would get busy, and the "Krumps" would come lumbering over, followed by snappy little "whizz-bangs" and then that elegant piece of parapet, that had taken ten men and a corporal all night to build, would go flying in all directions and the desirable dug-out, which was being erected to one's own specifications, would, in a flash, become a heap of lacerated sandbags, broken beams and corrugated iron, to say nothing of shouts for stretcher-bearers.

It was a very tired battalion that came out of the trenches on the night of August 10th and bivouaced close to the White Chateau at Kruisstraat, gulping down hot tea and rum out of enamelled mugs before lying down to sleep just as the sun rose.

Then stillness reigned under the poplars that flanked the bivouac, which was broken only by the twittering of the wakening birds, the desultory rifle fire in the distance, the snores of husky private soldiers, and the prattle of a newly-joined subaltern, so elated at having received his baptism of fire unscathed, and his ration of tea and rum unstinted, that he spent most of the rest of the night grandiloquently narrating to the transport officer the horrors of the Battle of Hooge.

August passed and September came. The battalion still held the same part of the line in the same way, but the atmosphere at Ypres was getting more unhealthy as the days drew in and the nights got colder. More "stuff" was flying about, and we find such entries in the battalion war diary as :—

"49 and 50 trenches whizz-banged during the afternoon."

"48 trench sausaged."

"Enemy shelled communication trenches 47S and 42A."

These simple phrases meant an uneasy life and perhaps an uncomfortable death. At this period the enemy "crumped" our trenches very heavily, and the sandbag barricades had to be be built up again by night, which entailed extra fatigue parties and a lot of very hard work. The railway dug-outs were also shelled, and the Boches put one large shell into the pond, much to the disgust of the local anglers.

But though the Germans were making themselves thoroughly disagreeable, there was one thing with which they could not interfere, and that was the evening sunset. And what sunsets they were ; fiery, blood-red, full of majesty, full of foreboding. Just as the men in the trenches were "standing to" the sun was going down behind the ruins of the Cloth Hall like some gigantic pigeon-blood ruby, and the heavens were filled with all manner of redness, pink, scarlet, vermilion, couleur de rose. Belgium could hold her own in sunsets. And sentimental Private Atkins cleaning his rifle in 47 (the international trench, ten yards from the Germans) gazed with admiration mingled with solemn wonder ; it was such a magnificent sight, but it was so awfully red, so very much like blood.

On September the 22nd the situation definitely warmed up. The artillery of the 3rd and 14th Divisions fired industriously on the German lines opposite the sector held by the battalion.

On September 23rd they bombarded again at 4 a.m. and during the day heavy firing was heard a long way to the south. The general impression was that there was "something doing," and there were strong rumours that the long-talked-of "push" was beginning. That night there was a thunderstorm and heavy rain, and the trenches became very wet and muddy and thoroughly uncomfortable.

The following day (September 24th) our guns bombarded again at 4.20 a.m. and orders were received regarding the next day's bombardment and attack.

At 4.20 a.m. on September 25th, after a heavy bombardment, the 3rd and 14th Divisions attacked Bellewarde on the left of the 46th Division's sector, but without much success, though they sustained very heavy casualties.

The 4th Leicesters put out straw in front of their trenches, which was to be ignited to form a diversion, but owing to the rain the straw was too wet and would not light.

At 6.15 a.m. the Germans began shelling their own trenches in front of 41 trench, doubtless in error, but at 8 a.m. the situation was becoming more or less normal again. It was now raining steadily and 150 German prisoners were reported to be passing Zillebeke Lake on their way to Kruisstraat. They had been captured by the 14th Division.

There was some shelling by the enemy in the afternoon, and in the evening Second-Lieut. Scholes took out a patrol from 47 trench and tried to find out the strength of the enemy in the trenches opposite. The patrol did its work well, and the trenches appeared to be very lightly held by the enemy at night. The casualties in the battalion during this day were one killed and five wounded. Information was received in the evening that the British and French had made distinct progress further south. That was all the news the battalion got of the Battle of Loos.

Next day the battalion was relieved by the 5th Lincolns, and went back to rest at Dickebusch huts. As the 4th came out of the trenches a heavy German bombardment began accompanied by sudden bursts of rifle fire and sounds of bombing. This was

E

rather uncomfortable and disconcerting as it would be such a nuisance to have to turn about and go back to the trenches to repel a German attack instead of going quietly out to six days' rest.   However, the "hate" died down, and the Boche remained on his side of No Man's Land.   It was only the Salient's way of wishing the battalion the "Soldier's Farewell."

CHAPTER XVI

A BREATHING SPACE

WHILE at Dickebusch huts orders were received that the Division was likely to move from Ypres, and all leave was cancelled. News of the heavy fighting and casualties at Loos came through. A draft of 35 men arrived for the battalion, ten of whom were found to be unfit and were sent to the field ambulance next day. Four private soldiers were tried by field general court martial. The Germans exploded mines under 40 and 47 barricade. The G.O.C., full of the joys of open warfare, visited the Mess. And the rain came down in torrents.

On October 2nd the 5th Corps Commander, Lieut.-General Allenby, visited the battalion, and Colonel Martin addressed him with much respect but no little vehemence on the inadvisability of sending totally untrained officers from England to battalions in the front line, quoting instances and drawing inferences ; after which the general congratulated the C.O. on the work of the battalion and wished all ranks good luck.

In the afternoon the battalion left Dickebusch and marched to Abeele to entrain. In spite of the long period of trench warfare the march discipline was good and nobody fell out. The train left Abeele at 6.55 p.m. and reached Fonquevillers, near Bethune, late at night. The men travelled eight in a compartment, and not in the usual cattle trucks. On arrival the battalion detrained and marched to Gonnehem, and went into billets there at 1 a.m.

The next few days were spent in route marching, physical training, bomb throwing practice, and interior economy.

On October 6th the battalion moved to Hesdigneul, where much the same programme was carried out. On the 7th the C.O. and the adjutant were summoned to brigade headquarters to discuss the proposed retaking of the Hohenzollern Redoubt. At 6.30 p.m. on the same day the C.O. saw the company commanders regarding this attack. From this moment the battalion knew that much would be required of it, and they realised that they had left what it pleased the G.O.C. (Major-General Stuart-Wortley) to call "this caddish sort of fighting," i.e., trench warfare, and were now going to experience the joy and glory of "going over the top."

They had become veterans by easy stages—Le Bizet, Kemmel, Ypres. They had always given a good account of themselves, and they were now really coming to close quarters with the enemy, and they intended to show the soldiers of the Fatherland

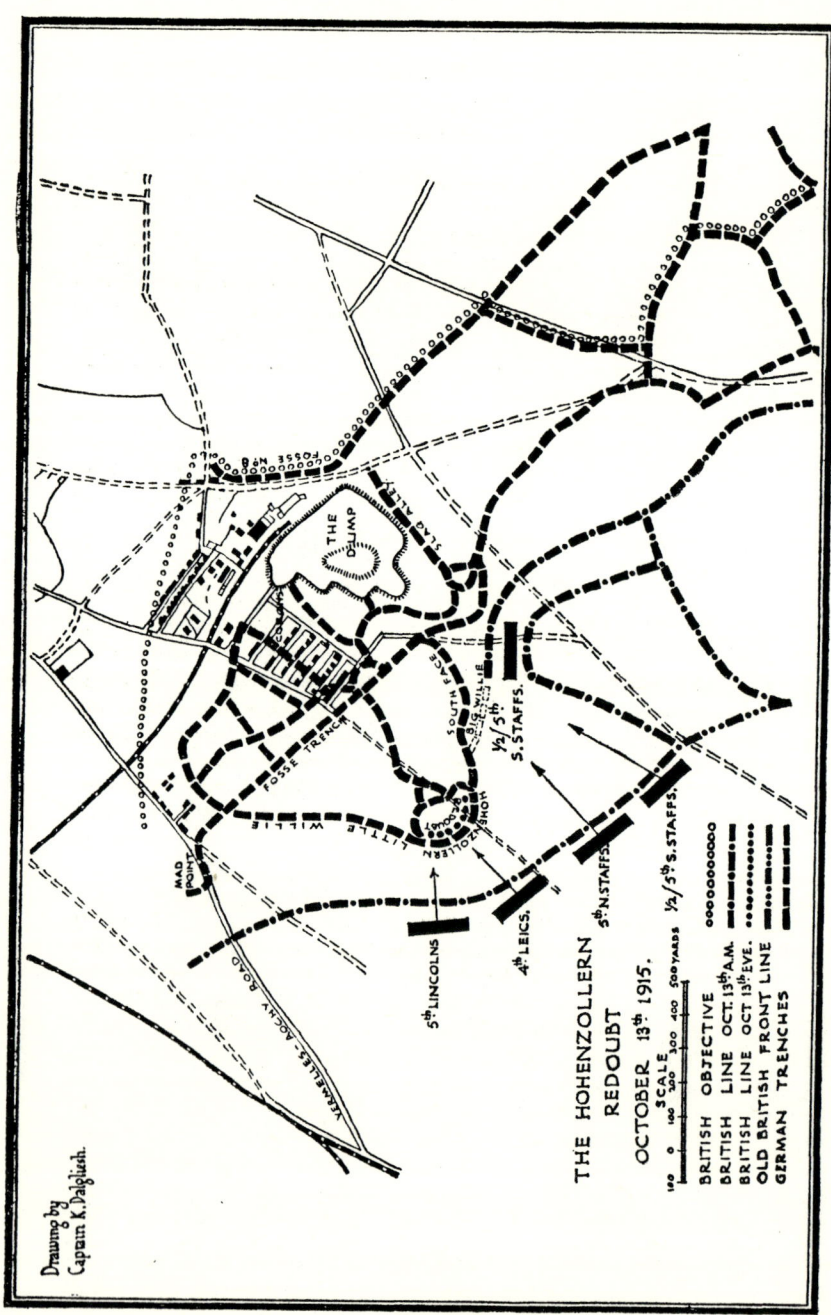

THE HOHENZOLLERN
REDOUBT
OCTOBER 13th 1915.

SCALE
100 0 100 200 300 400 500 YARDS

BRITISH OBJECTIVE ○○○○○○○○○○
BRITISH LINE OCT.13th A.M. ○■○■○■○■○
BRITISH LINE OCT 13th EVE. ●■●■●■●
OLD BRITISH FRONT LINE ●●●●●●●
GERMAN TRENCHES ■■■■■■■

Drawn by
Captain K. Dalglish.

5th LINCOLNS

4th LEICS.

5th N.STAFFS

½/5th S.STAFFS.

½/5th S.STAFFS.

S.STAFFS.

FOSSE No 8

THE DUMP

FOSSE TRENCH

LITTLE WILLIE

MAD POINT

HOHENZOLLERN

SOUTH FACE

BIG WILLIE

SLAG ALLEY

VERMELLES — AUCHY ROAD

that King George V, as well as King George III, had some "astonishing infantry" that would take some stopping.

On October 8th the C.O., adjutant and the four O'sC. companies went to Vermelles by motor lorry, and from there on foot to the "K" trenches, where by means of periscopes they were able to see a limited amount of the Redoubt, the Dump and Fosse 8. They returned to Hesdigneul by 1.45 p.m.

That afternoon the Germans heavily attacked "Big Willie" which was held by the Guards, who repulsed them with great loss, chiefly by means of bombs. The 4th Leicesters had orders to be in readiness to move at once, but not to "fall in," but as the attack was repulsed the state of readiness was cancelled at 11.15 p.m.

On the 9th and 10th all officers and many N.C.O.'s visited the trenches. The rest of the battalion spent the time throwing live Mills bombs, practising the attack in four lines of platoons extended to one pace at fifty yards interval, and in being shown by the R.E. how to reverse the parapet of a captured trench.

Church Parade and Holy Communion were held at noon on the 10th. At 5.15 p.m. all the C.O.'s, Seconds-in-command, company commanders and adjutants of the division met General Haking, the corps commander, at divisional headquarters. In his address General Haking, who had written books on military subjects, told the officers that the bombardment would be so terrific, and the gas so dense, that when the actual attack was launched the division would meet with little or no opposition in taking the objective.

On the 11th training and officers' conferences took place, and the commanding officer addressed the battalion on parade. Late in the evening orders arrived from brigade for the move next day.

At 9 a.m. on the 12th the battalion moved to Sailly-Labourse, where dinners and teas were cooked. At 6.15 p.m. the battalion marched to Vermelles where they took up stores and relieved the Guards in the trenches at 11 p.m. The trenches were good ones, cut deep in the chalk, and not the high command sandbag variety of Kemmel and Ypres.

CHAPTER XVII

ALL the morning of the 13th the battalion waited in the trenches. At noon our guns began to bombard, but the bombardment was disappointing. Was this the biggest bombardment of the war? Surely not? The transport officers of the 4th and 5th Leicesters sitting together in Vermelles thought the guns were giving short measure. Surely this was not what had been promised? The men in the trenches thought the same.

At 1 p.m. our smoke and gas started. The gas cylinders were at the bottom of the front line trenches, and the projectors protruded well over the parapet. Everybody hoped that as promised by the corps commander all the Germans in the trenches opposite would be asphyxiated or fly, and the rum was issued joyfully, lots of it. At 1.50 p.m. the smoke and gas stopped and the enemy began merrily to snipe the top of the parapet with machine-guns. This was not at all according to plan and quite contrary to what the staff had promised.

It is now getting near 2 p.m., the time for the assault. The trenches are thronged with men, everyone ready, everyone keyed up with excitement. They know most of the infantryman's art, these men; one operation they have never carried out, however—"the charge"; but in two minutes' time this will also be one of their achievements; then they will have performed the highest and they will know the worst. The little ladders are in position against the parapet, the seething mass of men is ready to climb up them into the open and into fame. The barrage lifts, a cheer goes up, over go the first wave; the colonel springs to the parapet shouting "En avant, mes braves"; the second-in-command (Major B. F. Newill) stands there, too, helping up men and machine-guns and bags of bombs. Up they come, over they go, forward towards their objective; no one falters, the position must be taken at all costs. This is excitement, this is history, this is life.

Yes, and this is death. The enemy machine-guns redouble their fire; the German artillery put down a barrage; the colonel is badly wounded in the leg as he gets out of the trench; men are hit on the parapet; men are mown down in swathes as they advance; down go the company commanders; down goes the adjutant; the second-in-command goes forward at the double, but the shrapnel catches him and he lies helpless under the German wire.

The third and fourth waves come on and meet the same fate; some get to the German front line, some get further. They hold on as long as they can but bombs and ammunition run out and their rifles become choked with dirt. Bombing goes on incessantly and there is some hand-to-hand fighting. C.S.M. Ford settles two Germans with the bayonet before being wounded. C.S.M. Hunt with a small party gets as far as anyone, but they have to retire as ammunition is exhausted, and the enemy are counter-attacking. All the officers are dead or wounded. Help comes from the 5th Leicesters and Sherwoods, but there is little more to be done. The attack has been carried out with the greatest dash, courage and precision, but the odds are too great, the machine-gun fire from Fosse 8 has been devastating. No Man's Land is a shambles.

The colonel stays in the front line trench ; he is in great pain but he still directs operations, receiving reports and giving orders. He reads the Bible to Clive Harvey, one of the youngest subalterns, who is mortally wounded, and comforts him as he dies. He remains at his post until ordered to the dressing station by the brigadier twenty-hours after the attack.

And so it ends. All the officers who took part in the attack are casualties. 188 N.C.O.'s and men answer the roll-call when the battalion is relieved next day and goes back to Lancashire trench. The losses are 20 officers and 453 other ranks.

In the afternoon of the 15th the remnants of the battalion return by motor lorry to billets at Hesdigneul.

The quartermaster and the transport officer mess together alone, but they dare not look at each other.

Congratulatory Order issued by Lt.-Col. R. E. Martin.

TO N.C.O.'S AND MEN OF 4TH BN. LEICESTERSHIRE.

The Commanding Officer wishes to congratulate the Battln. on the excellent work done by them in the attack of Oct. 13th.

Their assault was carried through with fine spirit and determination in the face of heavy fire.

The C.O. is exceedingly proud to have had the good fortune to command a battalion who acquitted themselves with credit when tested so highly.

(sd) R. E. MARTIN,

Oct. 14/15. Lt.-Col.

Extracts from the Field Service Pocket Book of Lt.-Col. R. E. Martin, C.M.G., written during the action at the Hohenzollern Redoubt, Oct. 13th/14th, 1915 :—

138*th Brigade.*

It is absolutely essential that more stretchers should **be** sent up. I have wounded men between here and the Redoubt who must be got in to-night. Please arrange with R.A.M.C.

(sd) R. E. MARTIN,

14/10/15.   *Lt.-Col.*

2.10 *a.m.*

Lt.-Col. Jones.

There is no one in the front line trench except M.G. Crews.

(sd) R. E. MARTIN,

O.C. 4th Leics.

2.31 *p.m.*

The attack was *splendid.*

I am hit in knee.

THE BRITISH ATTACK ON THE HOHENZOLLERN REDOUBT, 13TH OCTOBER, 1915.

(*Imperial War Museum Photograph.* *Copyright Reserved.*)

CHAPTER XVIII

THE END OF THE CHAPTER

THIS is the end of one of the chapters of the history of the 4th Leicestershire Regiment, and it is a glorious, if tragic ending. The battalion goes into action, fights to the death, and returns 188 strong having lost all its officers.

The Germans are a thorough nation. On March 2nd, 1915, 30 officers embarked with the 4th Leicesters at Southampton, and by October 14th of the same year but 2 remain. 12 have been killed, 6 wounded, one wounded and prisoner, 6 have gone home sick, 3 have been transferred: this does not take into account those who have joined in France and become casualties. Yes, the Germans are a very thorough nation, for the rank and file have suffered just as heavily.

And what a waste ! All these wasted lives ! All this wasted effort ! What has been held ? A few lines of trenches in grazing or arable land. What has been taken ? Not 100 yards of ground from the enemy. And yet they have perished, these men of Leicestershire. They were men who put duty to King and Country before everything. They gave their services and their lives while others were thinking about it and being persuaded and cajoled to join in the struggle of right against might, the struggle for the freedom of mankind. What a tragedy ! What a prodigious loss of life ! What a waste !

And yet it is written : "He that loseth his life . . . shall find it." And as there is a higher method of measuring effort and sacrifice, failure and success, than that generally adopted by mankind, Saint Peter, who was also courageous, flings open the Golden Gates with a smile of welcome, and in march this host of gallant warriors, who have given their lives for freedom. And, thank God, they at least realise that no man ever wasted his life who laid it down for his friends.

Three years later comes the sequel. On September 29th, 1918, the 4th Leicestershire Regiment forming part of the 46th Division crossed the Saint Quentin Canal and broke the Hindenburg line, taking 4,000 prisoners and making victory for the Allies a certainty.

The laurel wreath of the 17th Regiment of Foot is still unbroken. The sun still shines on the Magazine and the poplar tree stands by its gate like some gigantic sentinel in Lincoln green. And on the 29th of September and the 13th of October each year the Union Jack flies jauntily from the mast-head. But nobody takes much notice of it ; few realise why it is hoisted ; but there are some who look at it wistfully, for they know what a struggle it was to keep it there.

CHAPTER XIX

RECONSTRUCTION

AT noon on October 16th Major W. S. N. Toller, 5th Leicestershire Regt., assumed command of the 4th Battalion.

The work of restoring the battalion had begun.

The next day was Sunday. Canon Hunt conducted Divine Service at 10 a.m. There is no record of how many men paraded or of what the padre said. Probably an uncomfortable lump in the throat limited his discourse to a few words of comfort and God's blessing.

At 2.30 p.m. there was another parade. Lieut.-General R. C. B. Haking inspected the battalion and spoke to every man who had been in the fight. Alas, these conversations are unrecorded, but the General probably learned enough from the terse replies of these stolid British infantrymen to enable him to write an appendix to his pre-war book, "Infantry Training," giving graphic details of the effect of machine-gun fire on advancing infantry inadequately supported by artillery.

A decimated battalion is a sorrowful thing to behold, but it causes joy to the hearts of the enemy. A decimated battalion must be brought up to strength again ready to take its place in the line once more, and ready to go over the top when ordered. It is no use crying over spilt milk, spilt brains or spilt bowels when the Hun is at the gate. So when the General had talked to the men who had assaulted the Hohenzollern Redoubt he inspected a draft of 144 reinforcements which had just arrived from the base.

The 4th Battalion of the Seventeenth Regiment of Foot had received a shattering, but by no means a knock-out blow. The old spirit still remained, the new men were arriving. Soon they would be up to strength and ready for anything.

Hesdigneul was not a bad place. The bock was good as bock went. Four-and-a-half hours spent daily in company training and route marching was quite an easy life after what had been. Kit inspections, new clothing, stripes for most of the heftier privates, parcels from home galore. This was a gentleman's life to the erstwhile dodgers of machine-gun bullets.

On October 19th at 10.30 a.m. the Divisional Commander, Major-General Stuart-Wortley, inspected and addressed the battalion. He was tall, lanky, stooping slightly, red faced, moustached, immaculately dressed, brass hatted, with medal ribbons in rows. He spoke of the fight, of the past, of the future, in his easy drawling voice. The battalion then proceeded to company training. And in the evening the veterans regaled the reinforcements with the horrors of war, while the latter paid the maid who drew the bock.

On October 24th ten brand new officers arrived. They were Capt. R. Evans, Second-Lieuts. A. J. Wakerley, A. J. Tyler, G. Bolus, C. F. Wright, A. S. Neale, M. S. Holden, A. N. Coleman, A. G. Hyslop, L. R. E. Jackson.

Bolus, Neale, Holden and Jackson had all seen war service in the ranks of the battalion and had returned to England for commissions. They were the best possible fellows to train the battalion in its present condition. They knew its ways, its likes and dislikes, its tradition and its spirit. No praise is too high for the way in which they tackled the job.

The battalion marched to rest billets at Verquin on October 26th. The cushy life continued. Life in billets was pleasant. The weather was open. The chill of the morning air was exhilarating. The farmer's daughter had a pleasant smile. The human machine which had been tired, war worn and horror-struck, was getting back to normal English health and non-chalance. The military machine which had been battered, put out of gear and almost out of action, had to be reinforced and carefully welded before it was fit for work again. And the two processes went on quietly and pleasantly among the little farms. The working peasants ploughing and sowing their winter oats took little notice of the foreign defenders of their country. But they sold them café au lait, butter and eggs at a handsome profit, and secretly acquired socks and underwear of a quality far superior to anything they had ever worn.

November 2nd brought Second-Lieuts. H. R. Pochin and B. T. C. Gilbert and 108 men. November 3rd brought 10 men and Major B. F. Clarke, who took over command from Major Toller.

Major B. F. Clarke was a Regular. He belonged to the Leicestershire Regt. and had been serving with the 6th Leicesters, a New Army battalion. He knew his job. The battalion required an adjutant; he appointed Second-Lieut. A. S. Neale. It lacked a regimental sergeant-major; he sent to his Regular battalion for R.S.M. Richardson. In each case his choice was excellent. And the battalion increased daily in wisdom and understanding, and in everything that makes a battalion a joy to its commanding officer and a terror to His Majesty's enemies.

On November 6th the brigade marched from Verquin to Robecq and went into billets. Here the battalion began playing about once more with ball ammunition ; musketry and still more musketry was the order of the day. The new drafts needed it ; their acquaintance with a kicking rifle was very limited, and with machine-guns practically nil.

Also new bombers, signallers and stretcher bearers had to be trained to replace casualties.   Machine gunners also were manufactured ; in fact, their instruction was so fast and furious that one at least was sent to the base suffering from accidental wounds.

Everything was being hotted up.   Major Clarke was shaking the battalion into shape.   He did not fancy leading half-trained men against the virile Boche.   He expected to be sent into the line at any time.   He thought something was in the wind. Regular officers have a way of finding out things that are hidden from the wistful gaze of auxiliary officers.   He was right.   On November the 12th the battalion moved to Richbourg St. Vaast en route for the trenches.

Richbourg St. Vaast was a place of no particular interest except that it was absolutely over-run with rats.   Rats to the right of them.   Rats to the left of them.   Rats in the rations. Rats over the officers' baggage.   Rats under the quartermaster's bed.   One rat-ridden night in Richbourg St. Vaast was quite enough.

At 9 a.m. next day the officers went into the trenches.   At 3.30 p.m. the battalion relieved the 3rd London Regt. in the sector opposite Rue de Bois.   The trenches were a bad lot, very wet and in thoroughly poor condition.   But the battalion with its usual zest for work started to put things to rights, draining, bailing and sandbagging.

So, just a month to the day after the Hohenzollern battle, the battalion was once more in the trenches holding its bit of the long line that protected civilisation from the ravages of the merciless Hun (alias Jerry).

The trenches, though wet, were not unhealthy from the point of view of casualties.   There was sniping.   There was desultory rifle fire.   Richbourg was shelled daily.   There were the usual Verey lights at night.   Ration parties stumbled into shell holes and tripped over telephone wires.   Sentries gazed into No Man's Land, let off a rifle occasionally to keep themselves awake, and wondered what their young women were doing at home. In fact, the humdrum trench life had begun again.   Monotony punctuated by a sickening thud and then groans.   Hours of boredom broken by moments of bloody excitement.   Such is peaceful war.

Major F. E. Tetley of the 4th Lincolns was on December 1st attached to the battalion as Second-in-Command.   Once more the battalion was fortunate.   Good seconds-in-command are scarce.

On December 3rd the battalion was relieved by the 9th Welsh Regt. and marched out of the trenches.   All except "C" Company who stayed an extra day because its relief lost its way.   Imagine "C" Company's feelings.   An unnecessary day in the trenches.

It sounds little enough, but even after the passage of years one can almost hear the echoes of the blasphemy that rose from the throats of doughty "C" Company waiting in the dark for the relief that never came that night. One more day spent in filth. One more day standing about first on one leg then on the other and swinging the arms to keep the hands warm. One more day with that uncomfortable feeling that bullets are extremely near and extremely unpleasant. However, when they did come out of the trenches it was some compensation to proceed to join the battalion at Merville by bus, instead of marching the twelve miles on their flat feet.

The rest of the battalion marched to Merville. The men stuck it well though some had not got out of the trenches until 4 a.m., and the column moved off at 10 a.m. No men fell out. The march discipline was good. They ate their dinners by the roadside tired, hungry and cheerful. Every kilometre left the trenches further behind, a pleasant feeling even to the most robust fighting man. They could do with a rest ; they were going to have one. The December sun smiled on the weary column. The band of the 4th Lincolns met them outside Merville and played them through the town. Music hath charms. Packs felt lighter. Tired feet were forgotten. The R.S.M. swelled his iron chest. The adjutant's mare caracoled on the pavé. Old soldiers (aged about twenty) exchanged intelligent winks with the girls on the pavement. Young soldiers of the new drafts stepped out briskly to the martial music and felt slightly heroic. The 4th Leicesters had finished with the trenches for 1915, though they did not know it. There was a feeling of satisfaction and well-being in the air. They were a cheerful battalion and that is more than half the battle.

Merville was a good place. The billets were good. Life was not too strenuous. There was plenty of musketry and route marching. There was an inspection by the Brigadier (General G. C. Kemp), a sapper with bushy eyebrows and bright ideas. The afternoons were short. The nights were long. The battalion slept and grew fat.

Major F. E. Tetley came from the 4th Lincolns. They understand food in Lincolnshire. The Second-in-Command lived up to the reputation of his county. Aided and abetted by the quartermaster, he saw that the battalion lacked for nothing. They lived on fresh meat and fresh vegetables. They drank "ving blong" in their spare time. They forgot all about "Fray Bentos" and "Maconichie," and tea impregnated with chloride of lime. They felt like the replete Crusaders after the capture of Jerusalem that it was "God's own war."

On December 19th, a fortnight after their arrival, they left Le Sart, the desirable suburb of Merville and marched to Le

Tannay. Here a draft of 92 N.C.O.'s and men from the 3/4th Leicesters at Belton Park, Grantham, joined the battalion. On Christmas Eve, by way of a change and to show its tactical efficiency, the battalion did an outpost scheme, and then returned to billets to make ready for the morrow's feast.

Christmas Day broke on a very different battalion from the one that had attended Church Parade at Bishop Stortford Church a twelve-month before. Not an original officer of the battalion was there, very few of the N.C.O.'s, and only a few score of the rank and file. The tradition and spirit, however, remained. The battalion was still the 4th Leicesters, but with added scars, greater experience and more abundant laurels. The Hun had made a herculean effort to exterminate the 4th Leicesters in 1915, but as Private Hopkins playfully remarked as he swigged his Christmas bock : "It was na poo." The tiger's tail was still in the erect position.

CHAPTER XX

MARSEILLES

THERE is one period of the battalion's sojourn in France which will ever remain the most fragrant of its memories. It is the time spent at Marseilles. From a "bloody war," it became not "a good war," but "a lovely war."

It happened in this wise. The powers that be wished to send a division to Egypt. The 46th Division was selected and concentrated at Marseilles prior to embarkation.

The 4th Leicesters arrived at Marseilles on January 9th, 1916, after two days in the train. They marched to Santi Camp, five miles out of the city, and went under canvas.

What could they have wished more than to spend the winter in the South of France ? Was it not what the opulent did in the piping times of peace ? Shortly they would sail over the beautiful blue waters of the Mediterranean to Egypt, where they would live comfortably in Cairo with two or three "gyppy" servants, and take a lady friend out every pay night to view the Pyramids by moonlight. What more could the heart of Private Atkins desire ? In the meanwhile, the weather, which had been cold and windy when they arrived at Marseilles, had turned bright and warm. And the camp which had consisted of nothing but bare canvas tents and latrines had now become a camp fit for heroes to live in—thanks to the energies of the battalion H.Q. staff.

Life was very good. A little company and physical drill in the mornings was a fine tonic for the liver. And an occasional and not too lengthy route march in the afternoon was not unbearable and stimulated the appetite for tea. Another martial-cum-sporting pastime was to stand on an ochre-coloured rock, and, under the direction of Second-Lieut. M. S. Holden, the battalion bombing officer, throw Mills bombs into the Mediterranean. It was such fun to watch the explosion and then see the dead fish float to the surface bellies upward.

But the serious business of the day began after tea when everybody set out for Marseilles. Buttons were polished. Jackets brushed. Puttees rolled immaculately. Boots cleaned with infinite care. The trams to the city were crowded with highly furbished soldiery. The light of light adventure lit their eyes. They joked incessantly. They smoked innumerable cigarettes. Life was one long smile. And what did they do when they got to Marseilles ? The best way would be to ask some of the heroes themselves. History does not relate all their doings. Why should it? Suffice it to say they saw something of the life of the nation whose soil they were defending. They climbed up to the Cathedral of Notre Dame de la Garde and marvelled at the panorama of city and sea. They went to the Chateau d'If by launch and wished they had read "Monte Cristo." They viewed with much interest and some respect the Old Port, which has been a port for thousands of years. They sat outside the wine shops in the Cannibiere and drank bock or anything which took their fancy. They commented in robust language on the smells, the liquors and the women of the place. And then they scrambled on to the last tram to camp. It was literally festooned with soldiers of all sorts and in all conditions. The drivers in bearskin coats were phlegmatic; they did not seem to mind. What did it matter if a soldier or two fell off and broke a leg or a head. There were plenty more. Night after night the same thing happened with variations, and the Marseillaises stood quietly at their doors grinning and enjoying the fun.

On January 14th four officers from the 3/4th joined the battalion. They were Second-Lieuts. C. S. Beeby, G. L. Lea, H. H. Clifford and L. Paddon. On the 20th a draft of 111 N.C.O.'s and men from the 3/4th at Nottingham arrived. The battalion was getting up to strength.

At 7.30 a.m. on January 21st the battalion embarked on the Cunarder H.M.T. Aldania, 13,500 tons, and everybody was pleased. It was a comfortable boat. The men's quarters were good. Every man had a bunk. The officers rejoiced in comfortable cabins with sheets and stewards in attendance. The men, satisfied with their quarters, were more than satisfied with their dinner of soup with pearl barley, beef, haricot beans and potatoes, and rice pudding with figs. Atkins drew a deep breath of contentment, whistled softly as he promenaded the deck and, having poked his nose into the door that led to the engine-room, light-heartedly spat over the side into the dock. The war seemed to be getting better and better. It almost seemed too good to last. And it was.

In the evening, just as everyone in the Officers' Saloon was settling down to make a night of it, orders were received to disembark at 7 a.m. next day and return to Santi Camp. Blank, staggering disappointment! No blasphemy on this side of hell availed. No brandy was old or mellow enough to soothe the anguish. The rubber which had started so happily was left unfinished. The sheets, which had looked so tempting and luxurious in the morning, now seemed but part of a scheme of refined cruelty. The 4th Leicesters had borne the hardships, the weariness and the carnage of modern war, but never had they been called upon to bear such a disappointment. The visions of the Pyramids faded and in their places stood the Spanbroek-molen, Hill 60 and the Hohenzollern Redoubt. A mist rose before the eyes, and lo, the sands of the desert had turned into Flanders mud, and the blue waters of the Mediterranean into Zillebeke Lake.

And what was the reason of this sudden change of plan?

Private Atkins had it on the best authority that some very highly-placed, red-tabbed, brass-hatted personage in Whitehall had said with some heat that he "Wasn't going to have any more troops piddling round the Pyramids." Possibly for once Private Atkins was right.

The battalion disembarked.

F

CHAPTER XXI

BEHIND THE LINES AGAIN

THE evening of January 27th, 1916, found the battalion entraining at Marseilles for an unknown destination. The train went through Paris but the delights of the gay city were not for such as the 4th Leicesters. On lumbered the train, and after three nights and two days arrived at Pont Remy, near Abbeville. Here the battalion detrained, very glad to stretch its legs again and get back to rations more palatable than bully beef and biscuits.

The battalion marched to Buigny L'Abbe in a couple of hours and went into billets in farms. The weather was colder than at Marseilles, but now and then there was a touch of Spring in the air, and training went on with renewed vigour. The thought of Spring brought "Spring Offensives" to the C.O.'s fertile brain and, as any battalion that he led into battle was going to be an efficient one, the order of the day was "training and still more training."

There was musketry on the range. "Tip of the foresight in line with the centre of the 'U' of the backsight," "Press the trigger between the forefinger and thumb of the right hand," and similar phrases were drilled into the less proficient marksmen. But principally it was rapid fire ; every man had to be as much like a machine-gun as possible.

The specialists of the battalion were reorganised. Signallers, bombers, machine gunners ; nothing was overlooked, every part of the battalion was being furbished, practised and tested.

It is easier to train a soldier almost within sound of the enemy's guns than it is in England remote from war's alarms. The men realise very quickly that they are dealing with realities. It dawns on them more forcibly that a bomb thrown accurately at the right moment may save their skin and get them out of an awkward corner. They take more trouble with their musketry when they know the quicker they shoot a Boche in the head the less chance he has of shooting them in the stomach. Their instructors are practical fighting men and not theorists. At any moment they may be ordered to fall in and march off to practise their arts, or rather "do their stuff," in the face of the enemy. And so with the ardour and perseverance of their ancestors who drew their long bows at Crecy and Agincourt, they throw their bombs, fire their machine guns and fling themselves on their bellies to loose off "five rounds rapid" in the twinkling of an eye. To give their spare moments a brighter and more convivial outlook a regimental canteen was opened. Nothing like a well-run canteen to keep up the morale.

After a fortnight at Buigny L'Abbe the battalion mounted motor lorries at 7 a.m. on the 12th of February and went to Puchevillers and into billets.

The next day 400 men paraded with picks and shovels and marched off to work at constructing a railway. They were not told what the railway was for or whither it was going, but only to dig and throw soil, to carry timber and generally to do the work of railway navvies. This raised a good many blisters and a good deal of blasphemy. And the men who had volunteered for signallers, bombers and machine gunners were glad in their hearts when they saw 400 men march off early each morning and return weary each night, while they remained studiously learning the Morse Code, hurling Mills bombs and stripping the locks of their machine-guns.

There was much speculation as to the why and wherefore of this mysterious railway. In the opinion of the better-informed private soldiers it was connected with some "offensive," "push" or "stunt" which would take place at some future date and be carried out with such clear-headedness by the staff, and bloody-mindedness by the troops that, if they were not able to spend August Bank Holiday Monday at Skegness, they would at least spend it in some desirable billet on the outskirts of Berlin. And would have a couple of German prisoners to clean their buttons and draw their Lager beer, which would be much better than cleaning their own and swilling "ving blong" in some god-forsaken estaminet in France.

Two events of importance happened about this time. They were the advent of the Lewis gun and the "steel helmet."

The Lewis gun was hailed with joy. Two per company were issued. They were light, handy little machine-guns, and took the place of the heavier Maxim and Vickers guns which had been sent away to form the Brigade Machine Gun Company. The British Army had always been short of automatic guns. Nests of German machine guns had repeatedly held up the British advance causing terrible casualties. The Lewis guns raised everybody's morale. The Boche was now going to get some of his own medicine.

The "tin hat" was quite a different proposition. It gave the battalion a headache en masse. It was just one more heavy thing to carry. Odds were laid that those in authority would never swop their brass hats for tin ones. Atkins was annoyed; the thing was "a damned nuisance." It was not until the battalion went into the line that it realised that "tin hats" were preferable to broken brain pans. Then the value of this type of headgear was appreciated by all ranks.

From Puchevillers the battalion moved to Fienvillers on February 20th, arriving at 2.15 p.m. after having dinners on the road. It was a lovely bright Sunday morning and ideal for marching. There was some difficulty about finding billets for officers, but at last everybody was bedded down. Monday morning was cheerless, but the canteen opened in the afternoon. On Tuesday there was frost and snow. On Wednesday there was more frost and heavy snow. Winter had really come. But what did it matter? The battalion were comfortably settled.

However, an entry in a diary dated February 23rd reads :— "At 10 p.m. were told we were to move to-morrow. Damn !" It is ever thus in the British Army. Orders are delayed and issued at the last moment causing unnecessary discomfort and blasphemy. But the troops pass the starting point at the scheduled time nevertheless. The 4th Leicesters were clear of Fienvillers by 9 a.m. The roads were frozen. There was no time to rough the horses' shoes so they slipped often on the way to Montrelet, where the battalion went into billets after a great deal of waiting about in the cold. They stayed at Montrelet for five days during which it snowed and then thawed. Punctually at 10.30 p.m. on the 28th, just as everyone was comfortably asleep, orders arrived to move to Gézaincourt at 9.30 a.m. next day. Good staff work ! The C.O. rises at 6 a.m. The battalion moves at 9.15 a.m. Next day it moves to Doullens.

Rumours began to spread at Doullens. There was a transport route march under brigade arrangements. That began to look like business. The quartermaster looked more knowing than usual when the first batch of steel helmets was issued and said : "May be glad of them soon." The C.O., adjutant and Lewis gun officer disappeared for a couple of days on a visit to Souchez, a French part of the line. Then the whole brigade marched through snow to Sericourt, eleven miles north of Doullens. Obviously something was going to happen. "And about time something did happen," thought the battalion. Building railways was all right, throwing bombs was quite amusing, and tactical schemes were good fun in fine weather. But after all they had come out to fight, not to muck about behind the lines. The drafts who had recently arrived wanted to get under fire. They had heard such a lot about it from the older hands. They wanted to know what it was like. They wanted to know the worst. They wanted to be blooded ; besides it would give their letters home a more heroic tinge.

The C.O. noticed this restiveness and rejoiced over it with the adjutant. He in turn confided to the R.S.M. that the battalion would not be happy till it was in the line again, to which this iron-chested stalwart replied laconically, "Yes, sir. Do them a power of good."

So after thee days at Sericourt and two at Gouy en Ternois the battalion moved to Camblain L'Abbe. It was a twelve-mile march. There were continual checks. The road swarmed with hundreds of lorries full of French troops going westward. There were also a number of French guns on the move. The French were leaving the Vimy Ridge and the British were taking over. Camblain L'Abbe was reached at 3.15 p.m. on March 11th. The battalion went into huts vacated by the French. On March 15th it relieved the 5th Lincolns in support trenches at Villers au Bois. The battalion was once more in the line.

CHAPTER XXII

VIMY

THE 4th Leicesters had sat in trenches overlooked by the Boche on the Messines Ridge and at Hill 60. And now at Vimy the enemy were at the top of the ridge again thanks to those responsible for our shortage in guns and munitions.

If you had wished to visit the trench system at Vimy in March, 1916, you would first have arrived at the huts of the battalion in rest at Camblain L'Abbe.

These were not much to write home about. They were dirty because they had been occupied by dirty troops. For the French Army standard of cleanliness is not the same as ours. They do not notice little things like broken meats and garbage littered about. A dead animal or two in the vicinity of the men's huts does not worry them. And any old place is good enough for any old latrine. The French are great fighters, great thinkers, great artists. But collectively their proclivity for tidiness is not pronounced, and their sense of smell is undoubtedly deficient. Camblain L'Abbe was not a bunch of violets, but a sanitary sergeant and a few defaulters can work wonders, and did.

If Camblain L'Abbe four miles from the front line was not salubrious, Villers au Bois a mile nearer the enemy was far more uncomfortable. It consisted of support trenches and dug-outs which were the remains of a French camp. Filth, and then more filth.

To get to the front line there is a plateau two miles wide to be crossed, which is unhealthy as it is in full view of the enemy who can snipe with whizz-bangs. So it is safer to cross by a long brick-bottomed communication trench called the Cabaret Rouge (from an estaminet bearing that name long since blown to bits). The centre bricks of the trench have sunk so much that it is necessary to walk like a Red Indian on the war path, placing one foot straight in front of the other, a severe trial to the heavy-footed, heavy-loaded British soldier. This trench seems endless, but it isn't. And after an hour or more of discomfort, halts, trips over telephone wires and jams caused by stretcher parties, it suddenly opens into a valley, the Talus des Zouaves.

There is much to be said for this Cabaret Rouge trench. It is wide, it is safe, as communication trenches go. Of course, it is wet in many places. Its chalk sides are not revetted, and have a habit of falling in at untimely moments. It is the long red and white road that leads often to death, sometimes to glory, always to squalor and filth. But it is also the road that leads back to longed-for rest after much weariness, to blankets, to baths, to comparative safety, and to Blighty either on leave or on a stretcher. It remains in the memory a long line in indelible French chalk.

The Talus des Zouaves is not a happy valley. It takes its name from the number of dead Zouaves that lie unburied in it. They attacked with much dash and élan at the time of our Loos battle and managed to take the ridge, but could not hold it. They lost terribly, and their dead lie just as they fell in their red coats and white trousers which the winter has now turned nearly as black as their faces. Africa will never see them again, but truly they have earned a place in the sun.

The valley has very steep sides. This is all to the good because the Boches find it difficult to shell effectively. There are trenches and dug-outs on the eastern side for the battalion in support. They are good dug-outs. They would be ; they are old German ones. The Germans lead the world in dug-out construction. No waterproof-sheet-cum-sandbag-cum-cor-rugated-iron for them. They must have something safe, deep, roomy and well lighted. So the battalion in support lived in some comfort in the hillside, but outside the atmosphere was charged with the sizzle of sausages and the stench of Zouaves.

There was a similarity between the trenches at Kemmel in April, 1915, and those at Vimy a year later. Both were wet and under water in places. Both were disconnected, and posts rather than continuous trenches. Both were on a ridge just below and close to the German line. Both stank abominably from the filth purposely drained down on them by the protagonists of culture on the top of the ridge. And around both lay the dead soldiers of France.

Six days in brigade support trenches at Villers au Bois. Six days in support trenches at Talus des Zouaves. Six days in the front line. And then six days so-called rest in the Camblain L'Abbe huts. Thus was the line held.

It is unpleasant to get wet by day. It is perfectly vile to be out in the wet for six days and six nights, and roughly that was life in the front line at Vimy. Sandbags were filled. Trenches were drained. A good morning's work was done, and then "plonk" and a "sausage" from a minenwerfer would land in the middle of the trench in the middle of the afternoon. It was lucky if there were no casualties, but in any case it would take all night to repair the trench. "Sausages" could be seen in the air, which gave someone time to blow a whistle, and then everyone would dash round the nearest traverse for cover. We retaliated with trench mortars and Stokes guns, which were being used for the first time. We gave the Boche all the "hate" we could.

But there he sat at the top of the ridge with sausages galore at his disposal, and snipers with rifles with telescopic sights who blew the brains out of any head which showed over our parapet. Second-Lieut. S. F. Lennard was killed in this way. He was a fine young officer who had joined on mobilisation and gained much experience in the ranks of the battalion before receiving a commission. He was an officer the battalion could ill afford to lose.

Sausages, rifle grenades and snipers' bullets do much to make life unpleasant, but it is mining that really tests the morale. There was a lot of mining going on at Vimy. A mine going up was almost a daily occurrence, but not an occurrence anybody ever got used to. The earth shivered and rocked. Up went trenches. Down came sandbags, bodies, timbers, rum jars. Sometimes we blew a mine and the Germans retaliated. Sometimes several German mines went off as the result of our explosion. Mysterious tappings are heard or are thought to be heard under the trench. Atkins looks serious, whispers premonitions to his sergeant, asks which day the company will be relieved, picks his teeth savagely with a match, and has a peculiar feeling in the pit of his stomach. No one really likes living on a volcano.

It has been previously mentioned that the brigadier hailed from the R.E. Vimy was undoubtedly R.E. country, or so thought General Kemp. Visions of brand-new support trenches just behind the firing line grew in his martial brain. Almost every night he appeared at battalion headquarters and called Second Lieut. A. S. Neale from his guttering candle and stuffy dug-out. Out into the night they went armed with compasses and pegs. And under the stars or the clouds they plotted out new trenches. And Private Kenny of the sanitary squad marked out the projected sites with lime from a sandbag which he carried. Sometimes missiles from the enemy interrupted the work. And on one occasion, when shells were flying about, the gallant brigadier in search of cover flung himself into a shell-hole which was unfortunately full of water. A brass hat almost totally immersed in a shell-hole is an unusual sight even in the most sanguinary of wars. And from the sounds which immediately arose it was quite obvious that this highly-placed officer had, besides a vast knowledge of the use of demolitions, an equally far-reaching vocabulary of highly explosive language. However, it is not every Brigadier who will crawl round No Man's Land and its vicinity with a Second-Lieutenant every other night.

It was cold at Vimy. Goatskin coats were issued. They were the same kind of coats that had been issued at Havre a year before. They had also the same kind of smell. But they were warm.

Man not being an amphibious animal, trouble with feet soon

began. An unpleasant and dangerous complaint called "cauliflower feet" afflicted the troops. It was due to standing in water, and in several cases men's feet had to be amputated.

The work of bringing up rations and stores to Talus des Zouaves was eased considerably by a light railway which ran from Mont St. Eloi to the valley. Mules dragged the trucks and thus saved the work of carrying parties. Bringing up rations is never a pleasant task. It is one of the works of darkness. It is often the devil's own job. The enemy are well acquainted with the ways of ration parties. They have rations of their own to bring up. They know that transport usually moves up a road and that it must start after dark and be back before dawn. So at likely hours of the night the Hun plasters the most likely roads with shrapnel and high explosive. Then the terror that flieth by night descends on mules placid and recalcitrant, on transport drivers clean and lousy. It is no respecter of persons. And the mule-drawn light railway at Vimy echoes with the same snortings, the same clatter of hooves, and the same strange oaths that are heard every night on every road up to the British line. Many mules were lost on the way up to Vimy. They died in harness. They have no known grave. Nor has an animal-loving nation thought fit to erect any prominent memorial to them in its capital. Nevertheless they did their job.

So much for Vimy. From March 16th to April 23rd it cost the battalion 20 killed and 76 wounded, to say nothing of the number who went sick. The battalion never liked the place. Why should it? It remained a memory of mud, mines, stinks, and "sausages."

The French had fraternised with the Germans before the British took over the trenches. The Boche had come over in the afternoons for tea and a smoke. The French are canny people, and perhaps they thought that, while the Germans sat on the top of the ridge and had complete superiority of fire, it was just as well to keep on friendly terms. The 4th Leicesters had no wish to fraternise. They had lost too many comrades for that. And besides the brigadier would not have liked it. So they hung on to difficult trenches. When things were thrown at them they threw back as much as they could. And when the 2nd Irish Rifles relieved them eight hours late at 6 a.m. on Saint George's Day they rejoiced exceedingly. And they whistled lustily as they mounted the motor lorries which carried them to billets at Maizières. For sheer discomfort Vimy took a lot of beating, but it had hammered the division into shape. It was once more a first-class fighting machine.

CHAPTER XXIII

SPRINGTIME IN FRANCE

BILLETS, baths, bock. The battalion was once more in clover, or at any rate in straw. And a straw bed in a barn, even if it is draughty, is comfortable and pleasant after water-logged trenches. Also the worst farmyard smells are fragrant after living in an atmosphere throbbing with the aroma of decomposing Zouaves.

The battalion was very happy. There were wars and rumours of offensives. But it mattered little because the men had got it into their heads that they were out for a good rest and that they thoroughly deserved it. Although it was only April they felt that the summer holidays had begun. The trenches at Vimy had been notoriously bad; anywhere in the line they were likely to be sent would be more salubrious; it could not be worse.

There was a brand new draft of 93 men from the 3/4th at Maizières. There would be plenty of new hands to do the fatigues and guards, and to listen with open mouths to stories of mud and iron. Then there was a chance of leave. Seven days in Blighty. The very thought of it made life a wonderful dream instead of a dirty, bloody reality.

Springtime in France with all the hedges in bud; with the corn in the fields beginning to shoot; with a smart new jacket and a clean pair of pants from the quartermaster's stores. Ah, life could be very happy if one only looked twenty-four hours' ahead, and kept one's platoon sergeant supplied with cigarettes. The girl at the estaminet who sold the flamboyant postcards seemed quite friendly and had nice eyes; rather like those of the calf that had just been born at the farm. The tits made a lot of noise in the early morning over their plans for nest building. And there was one rooster who got up so early and made such a noise that it was a wonder the hens did not mutiny. However, it was Spring and the sap was rising. Atkins woke up and yawned and stretched himself, and spent a few sous on café-au-lait before cleaning his buttons. And when, after a hearty breakfast, he went on parade he heard so much about the absolute necessity of keeping the thumb in line with the seam of the trousers, and the horrible things that happened to private soldiers who failed to have their feet at an angle of 45 degrees when standing at attention, that he quite forgot that there were such things as trenches, minenwerfer and listening posts. He realised that the main purpose of the rifle was to bring it down to the full extent of the right arm at the present, and to give it a smart cant up with the right hand when sloping arms.

And so the 4th Leicesters became clean, smart, well-drilled, full of esprit de corps, and everything that a good battalion ought to be. There were route marches. There was training of all sorts. Bombers bombed. Machine-gunners looked busy under a tree in the corner of a field. Scouts crawled about on their bellies, peered industriously through field glasses to see if there were any brass hats or skirts in sight, and then studied the idiosyncrasies of the compass until tea-time. And as for the snipers, they spent so many hours of daylight turning the bottom of a dry ditch into a really comfortable sniper's post that it seemed a pity not to take the better-looking of the farmer's daughters to inspect it by moonlight.

Ten days were spent at Maizières with nothing worse than an inspection by the brigadier, and nothing better than the regimental sports. War was certainly getting more civilised. A year before at Kemmel no one ever dreamed of such a thing as sports. A trip to Bailleul on the company horse, or on a cycle borrowed from one of the signallers ; a drink at Tina's ; a bottle of champagne at the Faucon ; a bath and then a trot home. That was all the entertainment to be obtained for a battalion in rest. Now things were different. The ice was not so thin ; more troops were available if the Hun began to get offensive. The work of slaughter was much better organised. The waiting room of the lethal chamber was comfortably furnished. In other words there was a regimental canteen, a second-in-command who organised football and sports, baths in the vicinity, and a concert party within striking distance.

The battalion had a close match against the 5th Leicesters in the Brigade final of the Divisional Football Cup. The 4th won by the skin of their teeth 3-2. The adjutant did not consider it an engagement of sufficient importance to chronicle in the War Diary, but the rest of the battalion regarded the victory more or less as a battle honour, and looked forward to the day when the 5th might have a chance of their revenge.

In the middle of the regimental sports orders were received to move the next day (May 4th) to bivouac in Corps Reserve at Savy. There the battalion remained four days. Training went on as usual. The nights were cold and the ground hard. And the battalion was very content to shake the morning dew of Savy from its feet and march twelve miles south-west to billets at Le Souich.

Le Souich was a pleasant place. The billets in the farms were good. The weather was clement. The country was all spruced up in the green of Spring. It was a picturesque neighbourhood. Close by was the Chateau and Forest of Lucheux. The Brigade had the Chateau for headquarters. It was very necessary for the Staff to be quartered in a big house. There were spacious rooms in which they could exercise their great brains.   There was a park in which they could exercise their fat horses.   There was a kitchen in which their unimpeachable chef could exercise his culinary arts.   There were comfortable bedrooms fit for the reception of the tired limbs of Staff Officers when the toil of the day was o'er.   There was a quiet little room in which the orderlies played pontoon.   There was a cellar . . ; but we have gone far enough.   Sufficient to say that the Chateau de Lucheux was as good a peg as ever brass hat hung on.

The Forest of Lucheux was what really mattered to the 4th Leicesters.   They were soon introduced to it.   The very day after their arrival 200 men marched into one of its glades feeling very much like 200 babes in the wood.   The wicked uncles were there all right in the shape of a few nonchalant gentlemen wearing their hair over their ears and R.E. on their shoulder straps.   These gentry removed their cigarettes from their full-blooded lips, pinched the lighted end carefully and placed the unconsumed portion behind their left ears.   They then addressed themselves to the task of showing the 200 babes how to make wattle revetments, and what wattles to chop down. As soon as the wicked uncles saw that the babes were amusing themselves happily with the brushwood, they relighted their cigarettes and vanished, leaving the babes all alone playing innocently in the wood from 9 a.m. to 4.30 p.m.   Working under R.E. supervision was ever thus.   For nine days the babes played in the wood.   It was a nine days' wonder.   It was a wonderful nine days.   9 a.m. to 4.30 p.m.   Generally 200 men.   Sometimes 500 men.   It was a delightful way of spending the merry month of May.   The wood was shady.   The birds sang in the trees.   The bill-hooks whistled through the wattles.   Contented soldiers whistled through their teeth.   Wattle revetments were mass produced in the happiest factory in the world.   One morning the G.O.C., Major-General Stuart-Wortley, came and had a look at the work.   He approved, suggested and passed by. The same afternoon the Corps Commander, Lieut.-General Sir T. D'O. Snow, K.C.B., visited the battalion.   But the 4th Leicesters had nothing to fear from G.O.C.'s or Corps Commanders because the battalion was fit, and knew its job, and was aware of the fact.   The guard of one sergeant and twenty-three men it sent to corps headquarters was worth looking at.   R.S.M. "Ironchest" Richardson saw to that.   But nothing good or bad lasts for ever.   On May 19th the babes cocked a snook at the wicked uncles for the last time, collected the bill-hooks, packed up the hurdles, and left the Forest of Lucheux a worse place than they had found it.

Next day they marched ten miles east to Humbercamp, and went into huts.   The nearer the line the colder the feet.

CHAPTER XXIV

HUMBERCAMP

LIFE four miles behind the line is different from life fourteen miles behind. The atmosphere is not so bracing; at times it becomes positively unhealthy. The expectation of life is decidedly shorter.

One word and one word only dominated the air around Humbercamp. That word was the "push." Everybody was getting ready for it, everybody was thinking about it, everybody was talking about it, though in slightly subdued tones.

The brigade major had long conversations with battalion commanders. The quartermaster commented with wise nods and winks on some of the stores which were being sent up. The C.Q.M.S.'s passed on the ominous news to some of the more highly-favoured sergeants. The enemy seemed to scent something in the air and laboured unceasingly to strengthen their already well-nigh impregnable position. But Private Snooks was more enlightened on the subject than anyone else. For had not the dark-eyed, full-lipped girl at the estaminet informed him of the very day and hour at which the attack would take place?

The preparations went forward apace. Sometimes it was digging gun emplacements while the gunners watched complacently giving occasional hints. Sometimes it was burying telephone cables. Sometimes it was digging trenches. There were always fatigues of some sort. There were always rumours. And on May 31st, while the British and German fleets were fighting desperately for the command of the seas at the Battle of Jutland, the 4th Leicesters were providing a fatigue party 450 men strong to dig trenches preparatory to the Battle of the Somme.

At 3 p.m. on May 26th General Sir Douglas Haig, Commander-in-Chief of the British Army in France, inspected the 4th Leicesters in line with their backs to the hedge in a country lane near Humbercamp. He spoke to most of the officers and congratulated the C.O. on the smart turnout and soldierly appearance of the men. He realised that the division was ready to give as good an account of itself as it had done a year before at Loos. The divisional and brigade staffs would be almost the same, though, alas, there would be few of the same men in the ranks.

The battalion spent its time in training and fatigues until June 5th, when it relieved the 8th Sherwood Foresters at Fonquevillers, opposite Gommecourt Park. It was a nice quiet part of the line. The German trenches were about 300 yards away, which was a gentlemanly distance, and not like living and dying indecently close to the enemy as at Kemmel and Ypres, where some trenches were only twenty and thirty yards apart. Life was quiet, but work was hard. Saps were being made. A disused front line was being cleared and rebuilt. Bomb and ammunition stores and R.E. dumps were being constructed. June days were spent in perspiration in the trenches. June nights were spent in exploration in No Man's Land.

The communication trenches had familiar names such as Lincoln Lane, Stafford Avenue and Stoneygate Road. Once upon a time Fonquevillers had a church, but this was now in ruins. The crucifix, however, remained intact like many others on the Western Front. And as they passed by the more academic officers would say to one another, "Strange, isn't it?" And the less erudite private soldiers would grunt, "Damned funny it never gets hit." But some there were who as they gazed suddenly remembered the words of a certain company commander nineteen hundred years before : "Surely this was the Son of God."

Work went on. More guns arrived and practised on Gommecourt Park when they thought the Germans were working too hard. More officers reported. They were :—

Lieut. C. B. P. Peake, Second-Lieuts. J. D. Thomson, A. B. Pick, C. A. Payne, M. G. R. Elliott, A. W. J. Watts, A. W. Leslie, E. C. Doudney. Most of them had seen war service. They soon picked up the threads and the lice. They soon found that to command a platoon of British infantry was a hard job, but a good job, and incidentally a man's job. Therefore they were happy.

CHAPTER XXV

THE RAID

JUNE 25th found the battalion relieving the 5th North Staffords in the front line at Fonquevillers. It rained and it rained. Mud was everywhere. The communication trenches were little rivers. The front line was standing water. The relief was not completed until 2.50 a.m. The weather continued so wet that the great attack which was to have taken place on the Somme on June 29th was postponed until July 1st.

The attack at Gommecourt, which was on the extreme left of the main attack, was to be carried out by the 46th and 56th Divisions. Its object was to detach German divisions from the Somme and also to capture Gommecourt.

A few days before the attack orders were received at the 4th Battalion's H.Q. in the trenches to say that a prisoner was required from the trenches opposite for identification purposes.

The C.O. scratched his head and sent for the adjutant. Then together they did a little serious thinking, and a plan was drawn up for a midnight raid. Volunteers were asked for and Lieut. C. B. P. Peake, Second-Lieut. M. S. Holden and Second-Lieut. G. L. Lea were selected from many applicants. Then these gallant and fortunate young subalterns strolled down the trench to their respective platoons and addressed them somewhat in this fashion :—"The C.O. wants ten good men for a little job. He has asked me to get volunteers from my platoon, because between me and you he knows jolly well that this is the spot platoon of the battalion. It is quite an easy job, and more or less a glorified patrol, only we have got to bring back a prisoner, because Brigade want to know who is opposite. If we get a prisoner, as of course we shall, there will be a lot of D.C.M.'s and M.M.'s knocking about, and I shall certainly see that this platoon get more than their fair share. So those who want to be excused fatigues for two days and get a medal into the bargain can volunteer. I'm going and I know that you will be tumbling over each other to give in your names. There is going to be a lot of artillery support, and the worst that is likely to happen to any of us is a comfortable 'Blighty'."

The men were picked, thirty in all, ten under each officer.

This is the plan that was duly drawn up and explained to all taking part. The artillery were to cut a gap in the enemy wire, which was twenty-five feet thick. Peake and Lea were to take their ten men each, crawl up to the gap, rush in, seize a Boche and bring him back alive or dead, alive preferred. Holden and his ten bombers were to act as a covering party in case of any kind of counter-attack from the flanks. It all sounded easy enough. A good night's work, an M.C., and perhaps a spot of leave. Let the play begin.

The night arrived. The party paraded. The C.O. had a word with them. He said that much depended on their efforts as the identification was badly wanted. The adjutant looked them over. The C.S.M. dispensed the rum.

The party slipped quietly into No Man's Land. The night was dark and cloudy ; no impertinent moon peeped on the work of darkness. Everything was going well when the party was halfway between the lines. Everything was according to plan when the enemy wire was only thirty yards away. The flares were going up from the enemy lines just as usual. The sentries were loosing off a nonchalant round now and then. An occasional burst from a machine-gun in the distance broke the semi-stillness of the night. The party are on their stomachs now. The gap in the wire is in sight. The enemy are in complete oblivion. The flares still go sizzling up and bursting into radiance with a comfortable "plop." All is quiet on the Western Front, but in two more minutes some belated German will be hustled back to the British lines. And in a few days' time a red-tabbed, brass-hatted general will be distributing ribbons for heroes in a quiet village behind the line.

Crash . . . Crash . . . Plonk . . . Suddenly there is a railway train overhead. Suddenly there is a burst of red-hot hail. Suddenly optimistic British soldiers crawling on their bellies give a cough and a grunt and lie still. Others shriek with pain. The surprise party is surprised. And doubly surprised, because the salvo of shrapnel comes not from the Hun batteries behind Gommecourt, but from the British front. The men are bewildered. The officers are worried. This is not according to plan. However, there is the gap. The prisoner is there for the fetching. Shrapnel or no shrapnel the play must go on.

Peake and Lea urge the men forward ; now is the time to rush in though the alarm has been given and the enemy are standing-to and firing. Then once again the express train shrieks overhead and the iron hail descends. "Tell those bloody guns to stop," echoes from excited throats. But they do not stop. Over comes another salvo. Over go more British soldiers shattered by their own artillery. Half the party are now casualties. Lea and Peake, stomachs to earth, hurriedly confer. To get a prisoner now is an impossibility, for the gap which was quiet and open a few moments ago is raked by machine-gun and rifle fire. To get the wounded away in safety is now the problem. Holden gathers up the fragments that remain, and under his guidance the party haltingly retire bearing their dead and wounded with them.

Lea and Peake carry a wounded man on a ladder back to the British line, only to find on arrival that all his brains are shot away. They feel aggrieved. The C.O. and the adjutant are waiting for the party. They have done their best to stop the artillery fire, but their messages have arrived too late, the damage being already done. Peake gives the C.O. a graphic account of the adventure. Lea and the adjutant give orders for the evacuation of the wounded. Holden, dogged, weary, and bellicose, shepherds the rear of the party and is the last man into the trench. The Brigade do not get their prisoner. A certain battery commander gets "straffed." Lieutenant C. B. P. Peake gets the Military Cross.

The curtain raiser is over.

.   .   .   .

The Staffords relieve the battalion on June 30th. Gommecourt is attacked on July 1st. The attack fails. The 4th Leicesters are reserve battalion of the reserve brigade. They are not sent to the slaughter. The Staffords and Sherwoods lose heavily.

The taps of the Somme blood bath are full on.

CHAPTER XXVI

MONCHY AU BOIS

> D'you know our MONCHY AU BOIS,
> So charming, so je ne sais quoi,
> We've been there so long,
> And found it so bon,
> That we'd go back there any old fois.

THE verse quoted above is believed to have been written by Lieut.-Col. C. H. Jones, commanding the 5th Leicesters (as you were ! Leicestershires). He was a master of Uppingham (and Limerick). The lines give a rough estimate of what the men of the 46th Division thought of the Monchy sector. It was not too bad ; they had known worse ; in fact, they had almost a slight veneration for the place.

At 6 p.m., July 2nd, the 4th Leicesters received orders to leave the Corps line behind Fonquevillers, where they had spent the night, and relieve the 10th Loyal North Lancashires in the front line at Hannescamps. By 1 a.m. on the 3rd the relief was complete. It was a miserable night ; the rain came down in torrents. And suddenly at 4 a.m., without any apparent reason except pure ill-will, the enemy heavily shelled the battalion trenches.

The rain continued all day, and by the 4th the trenches were hardly habitable. These trenches were not of the sandbag breastwork kind, but were dug trenches. In normal weather they were not unpleasant, and there were somegood deep dug-outs. At Hannescamps 1,000 yards from the front line there was a bank honeycombed with dug-outs which housed Battalion H.Q. and one company.

Besides the rain and the shelling the battalion's discomfort was increased by gas. Not enemy gas ; oh dear no ! A new type of R.E. officer arrived, demanded access to the front line, demanded fatigue parties of tired men to carry heavy gas cylinders, demanded the use of the best dug-out and ordered the already crumbling trench to be cut about this way and that to suit his gas cylinders. What a vile weapon is gas ! What a vile feeling it is to sit in a trench full of gas cylinders, watching to see if the wind is favour-able to project the gas towards the enemy's line, wondering what will happen if an enemy shell registers a direct hit on a cylinder ! It is the wind that matters, but the "breeze" is always "up" when the "gas merchants" are about. And so from July 7th to the 9th the battalion lived an amphibious existence more or less surrounded by gas cylinders, listening to the rumble of the

Somme battle to the south, and pondering on the fickleness of summer weather and the turpitude of the once-respectable God Mars who had now opened a chemist's shop next door to his smithy.

Early in July Major-General the Hon E. J. Montagu-Stuart Wortley, C.B., C.M.G., D.S.O., M.V.O., relinquished command of the 46th Division and Major-General William Thwaites assumed command.

General Thwaites was a short thick-set man, of a build not unlike Sir John French. He was a gunner, and therefore believed in fat horses. He knew the ways of senior officers, quartermasters and transport mules, which is saying much. He would stand by the side of the road and watch a battalion pass. B. Company following A., and D. Company following C., and woe betide if, when the transport passed, B. Company's cooker should be in front of A.'s. A badly-packed limbered wagon, or a mule without a shoe, a field officer without the regulation holsters on his saddle bow, and a storm arose and the earth shook and even the stony heart of R.Q.M.S. Robertson trembled, just because a small man with a flush mounting to his red face pointed with a cane and uttered a few staccato sentences. General Thwaites was a master of detail. He believed that there was no such thing as a perfect battalion, squadron, or battery, and that it was his business to draw attention to any fault great or small so that the ideal might be more nearly reached. He once inspected the transport of the battalion. The wagons were clean, the mules well groomed, the harness in perfect condition. He looked here, he looked there, every buckle was fastened, every strap in place. At last he turned to the transport officer, who was rejoicing in secret, and with eyes blazing with wrath (real or simulated) snorted, "Why on earth can't you grow a proper moustache?" The T.O.'s chest sank to its normal size, and he emulated Charlie Chaplin no more.

On July 13th General Thwaites inspected the battalion while they were in rest at Saulty. He congratulated them on the work they had done at Fonquevillers prior to the battle of July 1st. He looked the men over carefully. He scrutinised the officers with the eye of a connoisseur. Everybody felt that here was a master, and though he might be a hard master, yet he knew his job, and that was what really mattered.

The next day the battalion went into brigade reserve at Bienvillers au Bois. Most of the time was spent on fatigue carrying gas cylinders into the trenches, which was a difficult job as the weather was wet and the communication trenches full of water. The Hun bombarded Bienvillers au Bois now and then, and managed to put one of their shells into the village well.

On the 18th the 4th Battalion relieved the 5th Battalion in the front line.   There was a good deal of shelling during the tour, but not much damage was done.   The weather got finer, and the work of improving the trenches went forward apace.   The C.O., Colonel B. F. Clarke, who had been unwell for some time, left the battalion for a rest on July 22nd and Major F. E. Tetley took over his command and his deep dug-out.   The enemy began to use trench mortars to some purpose, and unfortunately the battalion could not give them as good as they gave.   However, the work on the trenches continued.   Even the brigadier, who was a frequent visitor, was pleased.   Deep dug-outs were constructed which greatly delighted the 5th Battalion who came in to relieve on the evening of the 24th.

The 4th marched happily if not gaily out to Pommier a couple of miles behind the line.   The C.O. arrived at his comfortable billet in time for dinner at 8.45 p.m.   Things were getting more civilised.   The best people always dine late.   And Atkins and his friends found the cookers alight and a hot meal ready for them before they dossed down in the straw of their barns.   And the sleep of these shilling a day gentlemen was sounder than that of their friends who slept in sheets at home.   Such is the reward of honest labour in the open air in July.   They had worked like the devil, but they slept like the gods.

Life in divisional reserve at Pommier did not mean idleness. Two hundred worked daily on railway construction.   The companies bathed in turns.   And in turns fired on the range, which was good for some of the drafts who had just joined. The training of all the battalion "side shows" went on as usual. The company officers exercised the company horses as often as possible.   There was plenty of work, but the sun shone, the birds sang, Atkins smoked innumerable cigarettes, the battalion lost 5-0 to the R.G.A. at football, and the brigadier, having inspected the battalion, expressed satisfaction.   Such was life in the neighbourhood of Monchy au Bois.

So it continued during August, September, and October. A lot of shelling and trench mortaring.   An occasional raid. And every now and then a gas attack.   On August 4th, to celebrate the second anniversary of the declaration of war, the enemy opened a terrific bombardment at 3.30 a.m. and tried to get into trench 95, but failed.   The 5th Leicestershires, who were in the front line and whose telephone wires had been cut, sent up an S.O.S. rocket, and then every British gun for miles round opened fire.   The 4th Battalion stood-to in billets at Bienvillers au Bois for an hour and then returned to their virtuous couches in the straw in their barns.   The trenches were badly knocked about, which meant more work on the next tour.   On August 9th the enemy shelled Bienvillers, hit "A" Company's billet wounding five men, and burst a shell close to a platoon wounding twenty men and killing six. They also knocked about several houses in the village. That evening the battalion left Bienvillers au Bois for the front line, and this time there was no grumbling, the depressing feeling of the last day in rest was entirely absent, and they tripped up the duckboards to Hannescamps on the tips of their toes.

And so it goes on, day after day, night after night. Sometimes in the front line, sometimes in billets behind at Bienvillers and Pommier. A lot of work, but little sleep. A lot of cursing, straffing and grousing, but plenty of laughter. It matters little what you do ; it is the people you do it with.

On September 26th the battalion are busy at Bienvillers cleaning up and preparing to go up to the trenches, when at midday there is a tremendous bombardment to the south ; it gets louder and louder ; the heavies of the 46th Division take part. "Someone's getting hell down there," muses the thoughtful private, as he lies on his stomach in the field adjoining the farm, writing a letter home as is his wont on the afternoon of the relief. It is a lovely day ; the autumn sun pours down with kindly rays, not blistering heat. Atkins licks his indelible pencil and in the right-hand top corner of the thin lined Y.M.C.A. writing paper he scrawls, "Somewhere in France." The bombardment grows louder. Atkins cocks an eye to the south and then begins the time-honoured formula : "Dear Ma. Just a few lines hoping you are in the pink as it leaves me at present." "Wish those bloody guns would stop," mutters the scribe, "can't hear yourself think." But they do not stop. The letter at last is finished with :—"This is a quiet place, thank you for the fags," and on the back of the envelope are placed the mystic letters S.W.A.K. Then at 7.30 p.m. after a journey over countless duckboards, laden with anything from barbed wire to tinned marmalade, the letter-writer halts in the front line. Here he relieves a man made in his own image but belonging to the 5th Battalion. He swops a cigarette, argues in vain as to the whereabouts of the rum jar, and sarcastically congratulates his opposite number on being able to stay in the trenches for six days without so much as filling a sandbag.

The gun-fire in the south slackens. At 8.15 p.m. the word goes round :—"Thiepval has fallen." There is much rejoicing. Once more Phoebus Apollo goes west in a blaze of glory, but to-night he is not alone.

CHAPTER XXVII

"MARCHING THROUGH FRANCE"

On October 25th the battalion had a pleasant surprise; they were relieved by the 5th Battalion a day earlier than usual. No one knew the exact reason but on arriving at Pommier there were rumours that the division was going out for rest. At 6.35 p.m. on the 28th just after dark the 17th King's Liverpools relieved the 4th Battalion at Pommier. It was not a model relief by any means as the incoming battalion found it hard to find its way in the dark. Also a pack pony of the 4th Battalion broke loose from the Lewis gun handcart and bolted, causing much blasphemy and no little trouble. At last the battalion was on the road to Halloy marching by Humbercamp and passing the P.O.W. camp at Saulty. No one fell out on the march, which was satisfactory considering the battalion had been in and out of the trenches for some months with little chance of route marching. By 11.15 p.m. the battalion was occupying the huts at Halloy, and the men fell asleep weary after their ten-mile march. They were glad to be out of the line, but they felt that they had left a "cushy" part of the Front for which they had a sneaking kind of affection.

For the next two days it rained intermittently. The battalion got itself clean. Close order drill was practised; in fact, the reign of spit and polish had begun again. A draft of fifty-five men arrived who were quickly taught the meaning of the word "fatigue." Guns rumbled in the distance, but no one heeded them; they were too busy cleaning buttons or drinking "ving blong."

After a couple of days at Halloy the battalion marched eight-and-a-half miles to Bouquemaison, and after a night there another ten miles to Noeux, and the next day from Noeux thirteen-and-a-half miles to Oneux; this time the whole brigade marched together. It was quite like old times, when the brigade marched up the New Bedford Road at Luton. But there was a difference. Then war was a romance, now it was reality. Then the battalions were at war strength, each led by their drums and with the band in the middle of each battalion. Now the ranks were thin and there was but one brigade band. But the men sang, the transport rumbled behind, the R.S.M. stepped boldly behind the tail of the C.O.'s charger, and the brigadier drew attention in no uncertain manner just as usual to any faults he noticed in his command.

Anyway, it was good to be away from the stinks of the trenches, from the ear-splitting noise of the guns, from the monotony of sentry duty. Marching is fine exercise even when the roads are poor and packs heavy. There was an element of excitement in speculating what the night's billet would be like ; it was interesting to pass through new country even though one village was much like the next. The more it rained the more the men sang. And when the sun came out again everyone whistled and was happy. It is a long lane that has no turning, and at almost every turning there was an estaminet.

On November 3rd the battalion marched into Drucat. A pleasant village. Battalion H.Q.'s at a chateau. The men billeted in farms. The officers in billets much to their liking. Time was spent in parades of all sorts. Bathing and washing clothes. It was not a bad life. Plenty to do but not too much, and a little time off in the afternoon for hair-cutting, letter-writing, football, or "ving blong."

One of the flies in the ointment was the distance of the training area from billets and the time wasted getting there. Ceremonial drill and open order attacks were the order of the day, and neither exercise is easy. The battalion had much to learn, and there was a lot of "as you were-ing" and "do it again." And sometimes, when standing rigidly to attention not daring to move a muscle, or when lying prone in the dampest part of a muddy field, the thought flashed through the patient brain of Private Atkins that there were certain advantages to be gained by living in a secluded little fire-bay in a front line trench. Officers are not so particular, or N.C.O.'s so officious within two hundred yards of the enemy.

With the exception of two days spent at Domvast the battalion remained at Drucat until November 21st. The battalion beat the 5th Lincolns 2-0 in the brigade part of the Divisional Football Cup. The stalwarts of the team were Captain Nugee, Beckett, centre forward, Phipps, centre half, and Tommy Jones. The rest of the team supported them well and they crashed their way through to the final, when they were knocked out by the 5th N. Staffs 3-1. Excitement used to run very high along the touch line in these matches, and an altercation between the players and the spectators was not an unknown occurrence. Football probably did the division more good than anything else while they were out of the line.

One Sunday afternoon the officers of the battalion caught a 'bus to St. Friquier and attended a lecture given on the Battle of the Somme by a certain Lieutenant-Colonel of another division. Sunday afternoon has ever been a time for heavy sleep or light recreation, and it was with mixed feelings that the party arrived at the lecture. Afterwards one officer entered in his diary, "A most depressing affair, and many more of such lectures would turn us into confirmed pessimists." It sounds as if the gallant colonel had been telling the truth.   It is not always wise to expatiate on the mural decorations of the slaughter-house to those about to enter.

Night operations were carried out with regularity.   Even in peace time they are never a popular form of training, especially on early closing day.   Now with ground frosts, and the wind in the east they were still more disliked.   To put the lid on the whole outfit some bright-brained brass hat ordered "night ops." on the night of November 21st and at the same time ordered the battalion to move off at 8.45 a.m. on the 22nd on a twelve-mile march to Domquer where it went into billets for the night.   The men were very tired when they arrived and the billets were poor. However, they had come to fight His Majesty's enemies in a foreign land of their own free will, so they must not complain, but it was now quite patent to them that in volunteering to serve their King and Country they had also volunteered to be messed about.   The Minden boys, the hard-drinking privates of Moore's Light Division, and the Crimea veterans turned in their graves and smiled.   They could have told them as much.

Next morning the battalion was astir well before dawn, and moved off at 7.15 a.m. and marched in brigade to Boussiers, fifteen miles, arriving at 1.30 p.m.   It was a beautiful day, the countryside was pleasant to look upon, the leafless trees silhouetted against the autumn sky, the brown ploughed fields turned purple in the sunlight.   Up the hills wound the long column of tin-hatted khaki, up to Longvillers and Maizicourt, down to Beauvoir Riviere and across the river Authie, up a steep hill the other side to Villers l'Hopital.   Passed peasants in the fields ("always at work, those blighters").   Passed cosy little villages ("nice billets here, Bill").   Passed open-doored estaminets ("Why can't we stop and have one ?").   Passed the G.O.C. ("Press on your butt, and turn your head and eyes sharply to the right").   Mile after mile till midday, when the brigade halted and dinners were served from the steaming cookers which had been rumbling and lurching in the rear of the battalions.

Then to billets in Bonnieres which was a good village spoilt by having three battalions in it.   The next day the battalion had rest in Bonnieres and the publican rejoiced with an exceeding great joy.

On November 25th at the gentlemanly hour of 9.20 a.m. the battalion left Bonnieres and marched in pouring rain fifteen miles to Mondicourt, arriving in billets at 2.30 p.m., very wet.   The G.O.C. was once more on the road side and watched the battalion pass ; he certainly took an interest in his division.   The men's billets in Mondicourt were good, but the officers' were poor. The best billets in Mondicourt belonged to the A.S.C.

Mondicourt was less than ten miles from the Monchy sector

front line. It was obvious that in a few days' time the battalion would be in the line again. November is always a depressing month with the days getting shorter and shorter, and the nights colder and colder. If the 4th Leicesters had spent their time meditating on the discomfort of Christmas day in the trenches they would undoubtedly have become pessimistic in the extreme. But they had other things to think about. On November 30th there was a Divisional Cross Country Run open to all battalions of the division. The course was two-and-three-quarter miles and over all sorts of country. Each battalion was given twenty-five minutes to get as many men round as possible. The whole battalion paraded. All sorts of details who at other times were consistently absent from the parade-ground were there. The cooks who knew where the rum went that did not go into the tea. The sleek private soldier who opened boxes at the Q.M. stores and who never missed his "Nestles." The pioneers who dug pits and emptied buckets but who never ran. All were there. It may have been a ragged start but it was a good finish. By energetic whipping-up, physical and verbal, three hundred and four passed the post in the allotted time, beating the next battalion by 7 per cent. It was a great victory. The G.O.C. was pleased and so was everybody in the battalion. Lieutenant Hyslop came in first and the Padre (Rev. R. J. Lowndes) was second.

The previous day at Sus St. Leger the battalion won the semi-final of the Divisional Football Cup, beating the 5th Sherwoods 2-0. Altogether the battalion's star was in the ascendant; even the Corps Commander was satisfied when he inspected the battalion with the G.O.C. on the very cold and foggy afternoon of December 1st.

On December 4th the battalion left Mondicourt for Bienvillers au Bois where they relieved the 6th W. Yorks Regiment in brigade reserve. On the 6th they relieved the 5th W. Yorks Regiment in the front line of the Hannescamps Sector. The winter campaign of the 4th Leicesters had begun.

The amenities of Monchy au Bois in winter were very different from those of the summer and autumn. Snow was on the ground. Patrols in No Man's Land wore white night gowns. Shells only made little holes in the frozen ground but sent lumps of hard earth hurtling dangerously in all directions. The trenches were infested with swarms of hungry rats. Rat shooting with revolvers was in vogue among the officers. The men fixed a piece of cheese on the end of the bayonet and then pressed the trigger if a rat was tempted by the morsel. Many rats died in this way. There was a good deal of gas shelling and all ranks were issued with glass phials containing some liquid antidote which was poured on to cotton wool and sniffed in case of emergency. The entrances of the dug-outs were provided with special blankets to keep out the gas. As they were mostly deep dug-outs this was very necessary.

On December 10th Major B. F. Newill rejoined the battalion from the third line. He had been dangerously wounded at the Hohenzollern Redoubt in October, 1915, and had only recently been passed fit for general service. The battalion was delighted to see him back again. On December 4th Lieutenant-Colonel F. E. Tetley, who had commanded the battalion since July, went on leave. Since mobilisation the battalion had had several C.O.'s. Harrison, Gresson, Martin, Clarke and lastly Tetley. They each had their own ways of handling the battalion. Some were feared, some respected, some liked. Colonel Tetley was loved.

Christmas Eve found the battalion billeted in Nissen huts at Souastre. A Nissen hut is a semi-circular structure made of corrugated iron. It acts as a shelter from the weather; it keeps out most of the rain; it is far more comfortable than a deep dug-out; but it cannot be called cosy. Santa Claus probably remarked, "This is a rum place to spend Christmas in, but I've seen worse, and if you think I'm going to get myself stuck in your narrow iron chimney, well there's nothing doing." Christmas dinners were eaten on Christmas Eve, and the battalion gave itself up to eating and drinking and opening parcels from home, and sending flamboyant postcards of thanks. The guns rumbled in the distance, but the knives and forks rattled on the tin plates. The elbows worked overtime. And after midnight, when the children at home were sleeping lightly and restlessly wondering what Father Christmas would drop down the chimney, the 4th Leicesters, with stomachs full of plum pudding and heads fat with "ving blong," slept heavily not caring a "continental" whether Jerry dropped anything down the chimney or not.

On Christmas morning the battalion left billets at 10 a.m., and with the sun shining on the frosty snow-covered ground marched up to Hannescamps to relieve the 5th Battalion. History does not relate whether they looked up and "saw three Huns go sailing by," whether they sang any revised version of Good King Wenceslas, or whether they found that their tin hats had got smaller during the night. It is sufficient to say that at this season of peace and goodwill the 4th Leicesters went into the trenches full of fight.

At midnight on December 31st our gunners, filled with enthusiasm and possibly with whisky, fired some shells at the enemy. This brought immediate retaliation on the 4th Leicesters who were in brigade reserve at Bienvillers au Bois. One salvo caused ten casualties in "D" Company. Shells were dropping all round the billets and there was a general rush to cellars, though in some billets they were so busy singing in the New

Year that they hardly noticed the shelling. Thus the curtain went up on 1917.

The weather at the end of the year had turned very wet and the trenches soon got into bad condition and needed incessant draining and revetting. There was plenty of enemy shelling and Bienvillers au Bois had a rough time.

In No Man's Land opposite the battalion trenches there was an osier bed, which in honour of one of Leicester's staple industries was generally referred to as "The Hosiery Bed," and one officer was mildly reprimanded by Battalion H.Q. because he sent in a report stating : "Patrol sent to hosiery bed found no Boche to whom they could give socks."

However, on the night of January 4th Lieutenant A. G. Hyslop took a patrol of twelve men to the "Hosiery Bed" and captured five Germans, one of whom was an intelligent corporal. The corporal spoke good English and spent the night chatting to the C.O. and adjutant in their dug-out and drinking whiskies and sodas, but he was far too intelligent to give away any information, though he drank a lot of whisky. And next morning he went to Corps H.Q. with the reputation of being a stout fellow.

About the middle of January the weather became very cold ; it snowed, and then the frost became fiercer and a hard winter set in. It had certain advantages. Everything was frozen instead of being wet. The work of ration parties was easier moving over hard ground. But the nights were piercingly cold, and a sentry's life was not a pleasant one. Hot meals were served in the trenches, being brought up in the tanks taken from the field cookers. War was becoming more civilised.

Several drafts of men arrived during January from the third line. And Second-Lieutenants G. S. Anderson, R. S. Provis and G. P. Clay joined the battalion.

On January 27th one of our Nieuport machines came down between Hannescamps and Fonquevillers, and the enemy shelled it unmercifully day and night to prevent salvage. This was always done when an aeroplane came down, and many casualties were caused among rescuers and spectators in these cases. The best thing to do was to keep clear of derelict aircraft unless there was a chance of rescuing the airmen.

Bleak January passed without much excitement but frost and the usual trench routine. February was half over before certain exciting rumours began to be spread abroad.

CHAPTER XXVIII

THE TAKING OF GOMMECOURT

THE War had now lasted two-and-a-half years. The Germans were being pressed on all sides. Truly they gave as good as they got ; in fact, their casualties were less than those of the Allies. But in 1917 they were beginning to feel the drain on their man power, and began scratching their heads to find out how they could hold their line with less men. The obvious answer was shorten the line. This they decided to do from Arras to Soissons and to withdraw their troops to the Hindenburg line, which was an immensely strong fortified position which they had prepared about fifteen kilometres behind their front line.

About February 14th rumours began to get about that "the Boches are going back." Everybody was pleased. The usual tales about summer holidays in Berlin and Christmas at home began to spread like wildfire.

On February 19th the battalion relieved the 5th and 8th Sherwoods in trenches opposite Gommecourt, with H.Q. in Fonquevillers.

At 3 a.m. on February 21st the enemy opened a very heavy bombardment with trench mortars and shells on our front line occupied by "A" Company commanded by Captain Wright. The enemy then put down a heavy barrage, and it looked very much as though they were going to make a raid. Three platoons occupying the front line under Lieutenants Pochin, Mantle and Wordsworth withdrew or thinned their line and blocked the communication trenches but left the Lewis guns to hold the front line in case of attack. At the same time they asked for artillery support, and in less than four minutes all our guns in the neighbourhood were plastering Gommecourt. It was an unpleasant hour-and-a-half. If the Germans intended a raid none of them reached our line. Our men were very steady and the brigadier complimented them on their work. Two "A" Company runners, Privates H. Bradshaw and S. Coley, who had behaved with conspicuous gallantry in carrying messages on this occasion, were awarded the M.M. Later in the morning "A" Company was relieved by "B" Company who were in support. No one feels very brave before breakfast, and to be shelled unceasingly for ninety minutes between 3 a.m. and 5 a.m. is enough to make any self-respecting private soldier irritable. But "A" Company comforted themselves with the thought that the Huns were using up all the surplus ammunition in Gommecourt preparatory to recrossing the Rhine. The child of optimism is "morale."

After a rest at Souastre the battalion were once more in the line on February 27th and at 9.55 p.m. without any artillery preparation "C" and "D" Companies under Captains Nugee and Pilkington advanced by platoons and occupied a line of trenches in Gommecourt on a semi-circular front of about 350 yards. These trenches were based on the enemy's old front line. The operation was carried out without a casualty. Shortly afterwards the line was advanced another 200 yards. At 8 a.m. next day "C" and "D" Companies advanced another 500 yards, and occupied bombing posts at the junctions of communication trenches and the German third line. This advance took place in a mist which was of great assistance. "A" and "B" Companies now moved up in support, as well as the 4th Lincolns who had spent the night digging a brand new communication trench 200 yards long between the two old front lines. The front now held by the battalion was 1,500 yards long. The mist lifted in the afternoon and the Boches at once shelled the new communication trench, causing some casualties. They also attacked the bombing posts at the heads of the communication trenches, and in some cases drove our men back for a while. Continuous bombing and rifle fire went on all afternoon and through the night. But at 7 a.m. on March 1st when relieved by the 5th Leicestershires all the heads of the communication trenches were in our possession.

It had been a good show. The enemy had evacuated some trenches and had been bombed out of others. No Man's Land had been crossed without a casualty. And what a place No Man's Land was! The dead of the attack of July 1st were still lying out just where they had fallen eight months previously, and arms and equipment lay all over the place. The battalion had been lucky, for the mist had been a God-send. The bombers had come into their own, though they had to stand up to a lot of bombing from the enemy. It was fun throwing a bomb into a German dug-out just to see if everything was all right before going down, that is, if you happened to feel bellicose enough to enjoy that kind of fun. And after being sniped, machine-gunned, bombed, and shelled for two years the 4th Leicesters felt very bellicose indeed. They had never known the Boche on the run before; they had, except at the Hohenzollern Redoubt, never been into his trenches. Now they realised in what comfort he lived. What palatial dug-outs he had! How safe they were from shell fire! What a cushy life he had been leading compared to the life of T. Atkins, Esq., who with nimble fingers and a broad grin now pulled the pin from the Mills bomb and gleefully threw it down into the dug-out, with the time-honoured phrase,

"Split that among you, you ——s !"   But care had to be taken. There were many booby traps.   Trip wires at the bottom of the stairs let off bombs.   Things exploded under beds if anyone lay on them.   Mines exploded on roads if they were walked on. The old Boches had done the thing thoroughly.   They evacuated their comfortable trenches, but the roses they left had many thorns.   The G.O.C. complimented the battalion ; they had done well, especially as it was the first engagement of many of the men.

Until March 22nd the battalion were continually in and out of the front line in this sector.   They took part in no further attacks, but they continually expected to, and practised them behind the lines with much assiduity.   The trenches were always changing as the Boche kept retiring little by little.   The weather was cold ; there was snow, there was thaw, there was mud.   Stores and ammunition were carried up by mules many of whom died in the mud from exhaustion.   The villages had practically disappeared and were but heaps of stones and bricks. Gommecourt was an absolute wreck.   Douchy-les-Ayette had but one house standing.   Life was not unexciting ; the boredom of regular trench warfare had gone.   Semi-open fighting had begun, optimism ran high, but it was very obvious that the difficulties of breaking through or pushing back the German line were tremendous.   The mud was on the side of the defenders, who devastated all the terrain they evacuated.   Napoleon said :— "An army marches on its belly," and to march on your belly through two feet of mud takes some doing.   Still the days were getting longer, and occasionally they were fine and warm.   On March 10th Colonel B. F. Clarke left the battalion sick, and Colonel Tetley again resumed command.

On March 20th the battalion left the trenches at Ayette at 1.30 p.m. and marched through Essarts and Hannescamps and across the No Man's Land of their old sector of trenches.   The road as far as Hannescamps was very heavy, and it snowed from there to St. Amand.   The brigadier met the battalion at Pommier and watched it pass.   The men were wet and cold when they arrived at St. Amand, but Captain Shepherd, the Q.M., had cocoa and fires prepared for them, and they were soon slinging off their wet clothing, warming themselves, and taking more than a usual interest in the rum ration.

Next day was spent in cleaning up, baths, new clothing, writing home, and "ving blong."   It was expected that the battalion would be at St. Amand for a few days, so the C.O. and adjutant mounted their chargers and spent a pleasant afternoon looking at the training area, and allowing their fertile brains to ruminate on how they might put the battalion through the hoop on the morrow.   However, when they returned to their billet they found orders waiting to move as a brigade six miles south to Bertrancourt. At 9.20 a.m. the battalion passed the starting point. The roads were better than on the previous day. Altogether it was a good march. It was pleasant to be out of the mud and be able to stretch the legs. The company commanders dismounted at intervals and walked to keep themselves warm. The company wag, who was also a director of the rumour factory, advised his comrades that the battalion was now marching south so that they might spend the Spring resting in the French Riviera, and the latest-joined subaltern, who had recently said good-bye at Victoria Station to an extremely attractive young lady, pondered sadly on the fact that there was no mail owing to the move.

No sooner was the battalion under cover at Bertrancourt than violent snow storms broke on the village ; they had only just reached their destination in time. Word went round that there would be a week's stay at Bertrancourt. This was good news ; there would be time to settle down, and some of the inhabitants would doubtless be friendly.

Then later news was received that the battalion would move on again next day, but that was all. Consequently next morning was spent waiting about, everyone confined to billets, blanket wagons packed, billets cleaned up, no orders about dinners, and no chance of nipping down to the post office to buy a postcard. Brigade telephoned at 1.45 p.m. orders to march at 2.30 p.m. to Raincheval seven miles west. This time orders were given to keep two hundred metres distance between companies and transport. It was an easy march, no one fell out and by 5 p.m. the battalion were making themselves comfortable in good billets in Raincheval with expectations of moving again next day. The C.O., who had found a good billet, rose from his comfortable bed at 6.30 next morning and found orders waiting to move at 11 a.m. south to Pierrigot. Dinners were cooked en route. The weather was cold and bright but the roads very dusty. A lot of troops seemed to be moving about, which made the march more interesting when they did not get in the way. Pierrigot was reached at 2.30 p.m. Much to the amorous subaltern's disgust there was again no mail. The cat was now out of the bag however. The division is to join the 2nd Corps 1st Army and the battalion will entrain at Amiens. The director of rumours now informs the billet that the battalion is going north instead of south and that if the summer is not spent guarding the base at Boulogne (graphic description of the night life of that port) it will assuredly be posted to the Isle of Wight for coast defence.

Next day, March 25th, was mild, springlike and sunny. It was Passion Sunday. There was Church Parade at 11.30 a.m.

but again no mail.   The battalion explored Pierrigot, discussed the new summer time which had started at 11 p.m. the night previously, and wondered whether there would be any chance of a night in Amiens before moving north.   Next day at 1.30 p.m. the battalion embussed for Dury.   This embussing is a novel feature in warfare.   Infantry have previously moved on their flat feet, though a train full of troops rushed up from Ladysmith saved the situation at Elandslaagtre.   Wouldn't Hannibal have loved to come pouring over the Alps in charabancs?   What would Napoleon have given for a fleet of 'buses to get him clear of Moscow?   How Blucher's eyes would have sparkled as he embussed his Divisions to join Wellington's left at Waterloo by noon instead of by 5 p.m.!   Perhaps the intelligent private and the keen-eyed staff officer mused on these things that afternoon at Pierrigot.   Perhaps they did not!

From Dury the battalion marched to Saleux and were billeted by 5.30 p.m.   At last the mail arrived.   The billets were choc-a-bloc with parcels.   The amorous subaltern (as the Mess was cold) retired to a quiet corner of the nearest estaminet and read four letters bearing different dates.   Then he sharpened his indelible pencil, leaned heavily on the tin-topped table and composed a suitably affectionate reply.   A little training was done next morning and then every officer except the C.O. went into Amiens for tea and dinner.   After the rough and tumble of campaigning life the flesh-pots of the city are sweet.   A china plate instead of a tin one.   A trim waitress instead of a batman with foggy finger-nails.   A pleasant orchestra instead of a broken-down gramophone.   The smell of good food, the bouquet of good wine.   A bath with hot and cold water.   A glimpse of bright eyes and neat ankles.   This is life.   This is happiness. This is a transient Kingdom of Heaven.   This is the civilisation mentioned on the back of the war medals.   Well, it didn't last long.   The battalion began entraining at 6 a.m.   Some fellows had fat heads but that didn't matter.   They dozed and recounted tales of the night before as they bumped over the uneven French railway; they were happy; they had plenty to eat and plenty of literature from the book stalls of Amiens.   What did it matter if the journey was slow and the halts many?   They were in no hurry.   They were due to detrain at Lillers at 2.47 p.m., but from previous experience of French trains they knew they would be hours late.   Tea time came, then supper time, then midnight; they were still rumbling over La Belle France, and it was not till after 7.30 a.m. that they detrained at Lillers. The men had breakfast in a field close to the station at 9.30 a.m. By 10.40 a.m. the battalion were leaving Lillers on a fifteen mile march to Flechin in heavy rain.   But they marched well; a cramped day of enforced idleness in the train had done them no harm. At Flechin there were good billets for everyone. The only snag was that brigade H.Q. were looking for billets in the same village, and the battalion did not look forward with pleasure to having greatness thrust upon them.

The battalion stayed at Flechin for a fortnight. The weather was fickle; there were bright spring days, there were bitterly cold snow-storms. The time was spent doing all kinds of training. Route marching, musketry on the range, drill and attack practice. Lieutenant-General Sir Claude Jacob, the Corps Commander, inspected the division and expressed himself satisfied.

On April 13th the battalion left Flechin for L'Ecleme, a thirteen mile march via St. Hilaire and Lillers; only four men fell out which was not bad considering two hundred of them were wearing new boots. The day was fine and bright; the country was flat and drained with dykes. The billets in the long straggling village of L'Ecleme were not too bad. Close to was the village of Gonnehem where the battalion had rested before the Hohenzollern battle in October, 1915.

After a couple of days at L'Ecleme the battalion moved five miles to Vendin le Bethune. On April 18th the battalion marched fourteen miles to Bully Grenay and relieved the 8th R.W.K.'s in support trenches in front of Lens.

CHAPTER XXIX

LENS

THE best description of Lens is that it was "perfectly bloody." From the time the battalion relieved the 1st North Staffs in the front line at Cite St. Laurent to the time they left Lens at the beginning of July they always hated the place.

Before the war Lens was a small mining town with slag heaps and miners' cottages in all directions. Now the whole place was a chaos of slag heaps, broken-down houses, cellars, and shell holes. It was a rabbit warren infested by wild men who threw missiles at one another whenever they met or heard any movement, and savages who rushed at one another with cold steel. Never was there such a reign of battle, murder, and sudden death. The fight for freedom had been driven underground. Friend and foe were mixed in a welter of slag, bricks, and blood. Projectiles of all sorts came hurtling through the air and converted comfortable cellars into uncomfortable graves.

There was always the feeling of uncertainty. No one was ever quite certain who occupied the next cellar. It was the easiest thing in the world to lose one's way by day or night. Thus the underground battle went on continuously. The 46th Division put its back into the job.

On April 21st "C" Company of the 4th Leicesters attacked an enemy trench and took ten prisoners of the 93rd Regiment without loss. Two lieutenants, H. J. A. Parkinson and E. C. Doudney, with Nos. 9 and 12 platoons carried out the operation and did it well. Second-Lieutenant A. W. Leslie of "D" Company was killed whilst bringing up mortar ammunition to the line. He was a promising young officer and was greatly missed by all.

April 22nd was a dirty day. "A" Company relieved "C" Company in the front line, such as it was, in the early morning. Orders were given to take Narval trench which was held by the enemy. Two patrols report the wire uncut. "A" Company send a platoon under Second-Lieutenant Whitcher to attack Narval on the south flank. "B" Company send a platoon under Second-Lieutenant J. B. Lambie to the north flank. The trench is captured but cannot be held as the Germans counter-attack with overwhelming numbers. Whitcher is killed. Lambie is missing. "A" Company are heavily shelled and lose a lot of men. Second-Lieutenants C. D. Brown and J. Gemmill are wounded whilst reinforcing the attacking platoons. Altogether the casualties are sixty killed and wounded.

"All the officers, N.C.O.'s and men of these companies displayed magnificent courage all through these operations," says the War Diary. "Hoch, hoch der Vaterland," grunts the phlegmatic Bosche from his cellar.

Next evening after the sun had gone down and the evening "hate" had died away the battalion was relieved by the 5th Leicestershires. Back marched the 4th to billets at Bully Grenay leaving behind them a patch of ground illuminated by Verey lights and fires, shaken by explosions of bombs, shrapnel and H.E., and echoing with the iron stutter of machine-guns and the groans of mankind. Sordid industrial Lens had become a fiery, bloody hell.

The joke of the whole thing was that battalion headquarters at Bully Grenay were badly shelled and got a couple of direct hits. The H.Q. cooks and grooms did not think much of this kind of treatment so the H.Q. were moved to a less palatial but less conspicuous billet.

The relief was completed by 12.30 a.m. At 8.40 p.m. the same day the battalion was on the move back to brigade support line at Cite St. Pierre, a march of five miles. Everyone was tired. Five miles out and five miles back. Shelling all day and night. Frequent casualties. What a day and St. George's Day too! The dragon must be roaring with laughter and wagging his tail for joy. The M.O. fainted from exhaustion on the way back to the trenches, and M.O.'s are tough.

For the next twelve days the battalion was in Lens either in support or in the front line. The troops lived in cellars, carried gas cylinders for the R.E., watched aeroplane fights, listened to artillery duels, fought when necessary, groused incessantly, and died heroically.

The optimists on the staff who had expected the Boche to retire from Lens under a little pressure were sadly at fault in their calculations. The Boche intended to hang on to Lens, and did.

On Sunday evening, May 6th, the 5th Sherwoods relieved the battalion who went back to Noeux les Mines to rest. It was pleasant to be ten miles behind the line again. The billets at Noeux were good, so were the baths. The weather was sunny and hot. The enemy shelled the town a little but did not do much damage. Life was once more worth living. There was football in spite of the heat. A Boche aeroplane caused some excitement by shooting down an observation balloon, and the troops thoroughly enjoyed watching the observers coming down in parachutes. Nothing like a little excitement to dispel drab monotony. On May 11th the G.O.C. Division decorated eight men of the battalion, congratulating them on their conspicuous gallantry. The recipients bore the ceremony with manly good humour. They certainly deserved medals; everybody who lived or died in Lens did. Some puffed out their chests a little further than usual. Some wrote home: "Dear Wife, I've won a medal." Some drowned their new decoration in "ving blong." Some said, "Why should I have it and not Bill?"

The six days' rest ended next day. The medals were forgotten. The battalion packed up and at 6 p.m. moved up to Lievin to relieve the 6th N. Staffs. The day had been fearfully hot and sweat dripped off the men as they marched up to the line. There was a halt. The 5th Lincolns who were in front were held up by heavy shelling. There was much congestion. Congestion under shell fire is always unpleasant. A mule with a shrapnel bullet in its rump can cause considerable disorder. A whizz-bang in the middle of a platoon creates widows and orphans with sickening haste. This time, however, the battalion was lucky, there was much shelling but no casualties, and the relief was complete by 12.30 a.m.

Four days in the front line in the Bois de Riamont followed. On the 14th Second-Lieutenant W. A. Ferguson was mortally wounded and died next day. Everyone was sorry, for he was an excellent fellow in every way. On the 15th the enemy was found to be massing for attack south of Souchez River. The gunners were informed and got on the target straight away. There was no German attack. That evening the 5th Leicestershires took over the front line and the 4th went into reserve at Red Mill a mile and a half in rear. The next two days were cold and miserable, and the nights were spent in digging cable trenches. Then into the front line again on the 18th. The weather was hotter, and so was the gunfire. "C" Company's H.Q. were badly shelled and trench mortared, one shell exploding in the cellar and wounding three men. On the 20th at 3.15 a.m. two of "C" Company's posts were raided without effect, but six Boches were killed. "C" Company were not people to be trifled with even in the small hours.

Next night the battalion were relieved and went back to Red Mill. The weather got warmer. Meals were eaten out of doors. There was bathing in the mill stream. There were digging parties at night. There was fighting going on in the front line, but there was less enemy shelling.

On May 25th at midnight the 5th Sherwoods relieved the battalion, who went back to Petit Sains Fosse 10, which was five or six miles from the front line and west of Bully Grenay. The battalion bathed and cleaned up. Major-General Thwaites and the brigadier both congratulated the battalion on the work and fighting done while in the line. They certainly deserved some praise.

As an instance of the kind of life the 4th Leicesters had been leading here are two examples of recommendations for bravery in the field which were sent in at this period.

"No. 200500 Sergeant Worth, A.
No. 200300   „   Treadwell, W.
No. 200788 Private Kirk, C. A.
No. 201346   „   Whyley, W. H.

formed a rescue party to try and extricate five men who had been buried by a heavy enemy trench mortar. They succeeded in rescuing three of the men in the face of a very heavy enemy machine-gun fire. Their conduct was magnificent."

"No. 200846 Private Johnson, A. W.
No. 200724   „   Pratt, J. N.

These men by sheer pluck and initiative drove off a party of twenty to thirty Germans who came with the intention of raiding their post, which was a very isolated one. The courage and presence of mind of these two men undoubtedly saved their post from a serious encounter. They are deserving of the highest praise."

CHAPTER XXX

LENS IN JUNE

LIFE at Fosse 10 was not unpleasant. Certainly the place was shelled occasionally, but no one seemed to mind much unless they were hit. The powers that be seemed to realise that the troops had had a pretty good gruelling in Lens and that while they were out of the line they might be allowed a little real rest. However, Messrs. Spit and Polish soon appeared on the scene and there was a big ceremonial parade at Marqueffles Farm at which medals were presented, Captain C. F. Wright receiving the Military Cross. Afterwards the battalion marched back to billets and the medals were suitably wetted in "ving blong" or any other alcoholic liquid which happened to be in the neighbourhood. The night was spent in roistering, which was far better for morale than carrying rations and trench mortar bombs to the trenches.

It soon became quite obvious that very shortly there was to be another "stunt" which is a monosyllabic word for "attack by P.B.I. involving heavy casualties and obtaining negligible results."

It had come to the notice of the brass-hatted ones that enthusiastic British soldiers, who attacked and captured their objective, were often shot in the back by sly and crafty Germans who had remained secreted in cellars, dug-outs and shell-holes while the attacking waves passed, and then calmly sniped the attackers with rifles and machine-guns when the newly-won position was being consolidated. "This practice must cease," said the red-tabbed ones and thus the "mopper-up" was created.

The job of the "mopper-up" was to follow the attacking troops and mop up every German remaining alive on the newly-won terrain. Bombs were flung into deep dug-outs. Boches were chased out of cellars, Huns hiding in shell holes were neatly bayoneted. War is one of the games you pay to learn, and no infantry had paid more heavily than the British, but the lessons were at last bearing fruit.

So at Marqueffles Farm the brigade practised the attack first under the eye of the Major-General, then for the delectation of the Corps Commander. Every detail was carried out, even to a contact aeroplane flying overhead. The moppers-up annihilated imaginary Germans. The subalterns emitted suitable imprecations for the encouragement of their platoons. Assuredly the enemy would stand little chance against such a carefully prepared onslaught. Everything was ready. Everybody knew their part.

Every possible situation had been thought out and prepared for. The attack would be a colossal success.

Next day, however, someone in authority thought it would be nicer to have a raid than an attack so all the orders were cancelled, and all the sweat and blasphemy at the rehearsals at Marqueffles Farm had been in vain. Atkins was not surprised ; he had been messed about before, and anyway he did not like "stunts."

June 6th found the battalion in the line again in cellars in Lievin. Next day was spent in making final preparations for the raid. At 5 a.m. on the 8th our artillery began to bombard and continued until Zero hour (8.30 p.m.). At 5 p.m. the companies began to assemble in the assembly trenches. The 5th Leicestershires and 4th Lincolns were to go over first and the 4th Leicesters were to mop up. Everything was ready at 7.45 p.m. The assembly trenches were full. Then suddenly at 8 p.m. the enemy began to bombard. They had evidently got wind of the raid, some said from one of their aeroplanes. Fortunately, they rather overshot the mark, and little damage was done by their shells.

The assault began at 8.30 p.m. under cover of heavy artillery and a shrapnel barrage put down by the field artillery. On the right good progress was made and the objectives in Almanac Trench were reached. "B" Company under Captain J. G. Abell and "C" Company under Lieutenant Hyslop began "mopping up." They found a large number of the enemy in Fosse 3 where there were eleven buildings with many dug-outs. These were dealt with with bombs and mobile charges. Heavy casualties were inflicted upon the enemy and two officers and twelve other ranks taken prisoners. "C" Company had a lot of trouble with uncut wire and a machine-gun. One machine-gun cunningly placed and stoutly manned can knock hell out of advancing infantry, and often did.

On the left "D" Company met with serious opposition in Ahead Trench. They were mopping up for the 4th Lincolnshire Regiment and they suffered many casualties including their commander, Captain Wakerley, who was killed. Here again enemy trenches were entered, dug-outs bombed, and heavy casualties inflicted. The Hun had a very disturbed night.

The withdrawal began at 1 a.m. and the companies were back in their cellars at Lievin at 3 a.m. licking their wounds and lapping up their rum. Second-Lieutenants R. F. Wagstaff, E. C. Doudney, J. Douglas, D. T. Sloper and H. J. A. Parkinson were wounded. There were seventy other ranks killed and wounded.

The whole operation was considered a great success as many Huns had been killed and their dug-outs had been badly knocked about. The "moppers-up" had done their work with ruthless efficiency and the whole operation was a shining example of how a large scale raid should be done.

Next day was spent in support. The C.O. and adjutant got busy sending in recommendations to brigade for bravery and good work. Second-Lieutenant R. Provis was recommended for the Military Cross. That evening the C.O. (Lt.-Col. F. E. Tetley) went on ten days' leave to England. It was well deserved and so was the D.S.O. he received at Buckingham Palace before he returned.

It was not until June 22nd that the battalion got out of the line and went to rest billets at Bouvigny Boyeffles. Here they spent five days of hot weather, bathing, cleaning up, being decorated for the last show, and getting ready for the next. The G.O.C. congratulated the battalion for its stout work on the night of June 8th/9th and presented the M.M. to Sergeant H. Dixon and Lance-Corporal Bradshaw, and a bar to the M.M. to Private Price.

Meanwhile attack practices had been taking place at Marqueffles Farm in preparation for an attack on Hill 65. This kept everybody busy, as orders with regard to the attack were constantly being altered.

On June 27th the battalion relieved the 5th Lincolns in the trenches at the foot of Hill 65. The 5th Leicestershires were on the right and the 5th South Staffords on the left. The attack was to be made from this position.

The final preparations for the assault were made the next day. Stores of bombs and S.A.A. were brought up. Zero hour was 7.10 p.m. at which time there was a tremendous thundershower. This gave the attacking troops an excellent opportunity of getting out of their trenches unnoticed. The rain then stopped and under cover of a heavy barrage the attacking waves advanced over the hill in splendid order, and gained their objectives with practically no opposition, though a few of the enemy were seen to be running away, a most refreshing sight. "A" Company under Captain Wright and "C" under Captain Nugee were the assaulting companies. "B" Company under Second-Lieutenant R. Provis carried stores for both companies, and "D" Company under Second-Lieutenant A. B. Pick was in support. The captured trenches were found to be almost destroyed by the bombardment. So posts were organised and the companies dug themselves in for protection against shell fire which continued day and night.

Communication to battalion H.Q. was extremely difficult and information was carried entirely by runners who did their work magnificently, but on this occasion no communication by day was possible.

During June 29th the battalion consolidated their position

and were constantly shelled. They were relieved by the 5th Lincolns on the 30th, who were to attack at dawn on July 1st. It was a difficult relief, but was successfully carried out. All reliefs are difficult, but when newly-won ground is being taken over from troops who have only held it for a few hours and know little more about the terrain than the troops relieving them it is an unpleasant and nerve-racking business. Flanks may be in the air ; there may or may not be a good supply of S.A.A. and bombs. It is a question of hanging on by the eyebrows, and making tired men dig till they are ready to drop, and then expect them to repel an attack at any moment.

The 5th Lincolns attacked at dawn as ordered but they came up against uncut wire and machine-guns and so could not achieve the whole of their objective. The 4th Leicesters in support supplied carrying parties for this attack and relieved the 5th Lincolns at 4.20 a.m. on July 2nd. This relief was even more difficult than the previous one owing to the general lack of knowledge of the whereabouts of the posts to be relieved.

The fighting had taken place at the Cité du Moulin, which was rows of miners' cottages. It was a case of hiding in cellars, fighting at street corners, and sniping from windows. It was almost impossible to keep any good system of communication. On July 2nd no messages got through from the companies in the front line to battalion H.Q. until 4.30 p.m. and then they were brought by a runner.

As a rule a runner's life was not a long one and it was not unexciting. No one knows except the runners themselves with what risks they had to contend. Dodging from shell hole to shell hole, up one street and down another. Waiting for a barrage to lift, and then be caught by a worse one. Sniped at by whizz-bangs and machine-guns. Diving headlong into shell holes. Bolting into cellars. The life they led was not worth living ; they soon found that out and they cared little whether they lived or died. What they did care about was getting their messages through. That was a point of honour. Everything depends on communication ; they knew that. They knew that they were a tiny cog in a gigantic machine, and that if that cog broke down the whole machine was in danger. So they toiled and sweated, and dodged, and lay doggo. They were on friendly terms with the adjutant ; they even dared to chip the R.S.M. They slept when they could ; they gambled when they got the chance ; they had ready access to the rum jar (and they needed it). But they were there when they were wanted, and if Saint Paul had gone through half the perils that they went through there would be a few more of his scintillating chapters in the New Testament. Here are four of their names : Snow, Hopkins, Cansick, Felstead.

If it had not been for men of their mettle Leicester might now have a burgomaster instead of a Lord Mayor.

Captain .S. Pilkington and C.S.M. Osborne were killed on July 2nd. It was like Lens having a last angry kick at the battalion before it left the district, for it was relieved by the 25th Canadians at 9.30 p.m. on that day. At 4.30 a.m. on the 3rd it embussed at Aix Noulette and started off in clouds of dust to rest billets at Monchy Breton. It was a lovely day, and it was good to shake off the dust of unlovely Lens. Companies were only two platoons strong owing to casualties.

One platoon of "D" Company for some reason or other was not relieved and was left in Lens. Second-Lieutenant R. H. Bowell, who was in command of the platoon, however, rose gallantly to the occasion. Here is the official account of what happened :—

"Second-Lieutenant R. H. Bowell awarded the D.S.O. for gallantry and conspicuous devotion to duty from the 1st July to 5th July. This officer was in command of two platoons in the outpost line before the Cite du Moulin, S.W. of Lens. Owing to the death of his Company Commander and Company Sergeant Major, the only two who knew Second-Lieutenant Bowell's dispositions, on the evening of July 2nd he was not relieved. Although he knew that relief was to take place on the night of 2nd/3rd July, he remained on his line of posts until the 5th July, without food or water, waiting for relief and unable to get in touch with any other troops. He repelled several raids on his posts during this period and accounted for several of the enemy. On the 5th July, when nearly surrounded by the enemy, and his men being so exhausted, he decided to withdraw. This he accomplished successfully, and without sustaining any casualties. He reported his withdrawal to the O.C. in the line in a very exhausted condition. His courage, endurance and devotion to duty were beyond praise."

That is the way the Leicesters fought at Lens.

CHAPTER XXXI

MONCHY BRETON

AT last the battalion had a rest, and it was not before it was due. Everyone was tired and overworked from the C.O. downwards. The first day or two were spent in cleaning up and reorganising. Then physical drill and rifle exercises, and the usual behind-the-line routine. However, the weather was good and the food was plentiful. A lot of time was spent on the range at Rocourt firing the preliminary practices for the Divisional Rifle Meeting which was the one item of real importance looming on the horizon.

On July 8th there was a Brigade Church Parade near Rocourt which General Thwaites attended. Afterwards he presented medal ribbons for gallantry at Lens. Second-Lieutenant R. S. Provis received the M.C. He thoroughly deserved it. The G.O.C. said he was "proud to command such troops," which was not surprising considering the show they had put up at Lens. Then the battalions marched off to their billets with their heads and tails erect. Praise had belched from the lips which had often fulminated censure. That was enough. The men were happy. The ranks were thin but that did not bother them. They did not think of ragged bundles of flesh and clothing that once were men lying about the ruins of Lens. No, they were good private soldiers. They knew that private soldiers are not paid to think, but to do as they are told. Was not this the doctrine taught by the "Little Corporal" and also by their platoon sergeant? So they marched off parade as gaily as their heavy ammunition boots would allow. Then they filled their stomachs with ample rations of meat and fresh vegetables, and in the afternoon delighted their souls with the one thing that really matters to the British nation—football. The G.O.C. smiled beneath his iron-grey moustache. He had got his men (what were left of them) just where he wanted them. As George Robey would say, "What was there was good."

The battalion was at Monchy Breton and Orlencourt, the next village, for nearly three weeks. Life was pleasant. The battalion sports were a great success; the brigadier, General F. Rowley, presented the prizes. The battalion was inspected by the brigadier, and also by the G.O.C. Division and the Army Commander. It came through these ordeals unscathed, but much time was spent in drill, blasphemy, and spit and polish to attain the required results.

The Divisional Rifle Meeting at Rocourt took up a good deal

of time. The 5th Leicestershires covered themselves with glory and won the G.O.C.'s Cup, and that evening they filled it to some purpose.

The next day, July 21st, the battalion left Monchy Breton at 9 a.m. and marched twelve miles to Vaudricourt arriving at 2 p.m. Everything went well on the march till a steep hill at Houdain was reached. The weather was swelteringly hot and sixty men fell out on the hill. No one fell out before or after this hill. These stragglers were collected by the energetic Second-Lieutenant Bowell and brought on to billets. It was a bad hill and curiously enough the 5th Leicestershires found it even more difficult, especially as the flush of the previous day's victory and night's celebration was beginning to wear off.

After a night in comfortable billets at Vaudricourt the battalion moved to huts at Noeux les Mines. This was getting back to the fighting line. The officers reconnoitred the line at Hulluch which the battalion was to take over. It was a rabbit warren of tunnels, intermittently lit by electric light. These tunnels were safe, but unsavoury and festooned with fungus. The entrances of the tunnels facing the enemy were held during the day and at night trenches in their vicinity were occupied. It was a safe kind of war compared to Lens, and casualties in the front line were few. The battalion relieved the 5th Leicestershires in this part of the line on July 28th. On this date Colonel Tetley left the battalion sick, and Major T. P. Fielding Johnson took command temporarily until Lieutenant-Colonel J. R. Robertson took over on August 6th.

Now began the fourth year of the war. Old soldiers averred that the last seven years would be the worst, but through the minds of the most energetic and bellicose flashed the thought, "Will it ever end?" The weather was hot, but sometimes at night there was a touch of autumn in the air which brought a twinge to old wounds and a distant shivering thought of Christmas in the trenches.

From August 3rd to 16th the battalion were in divisional reserve at Vaudricourt. Things were peaceful there. The battalion trained as was their wont behind the line. The drums were reformed, which pleased everybody especially the sergeant drummer. There is nothing like spitting down copper and beating on a dead ass's skin to raise morale. It was a trick played by the Israelites, Alexander the Great, Frederick the Great, and General Booth. So General Thwaites smiled once more and gave the drums his blessing; he knew that Atkins was but a child and that children like blowing trumpets and beating drums. And if any man think that he can withstand the call of the bugle and the beat of the drum let him first make quite certain that he is a man.

On August 16th/17th the battalion relieved the 7th Sherwoods in the St. Elie left sector close to Hulluch and they remained in this part of the line for the next three months.

So August passed. Sometimes the battalion was in the front line, sometimes in support at Philosophe. They saw the 5th Leicestershires do a raid at Hulluch on the night of August 17th/18th. Captain Hyslop and Major Newill were wounded during this month and Captain A. S. Neale went on leave to England. September came with colder nights and shorter days. The trench routine went on as usual. Days of rest at Philosophe were marred by working parties at night.

On September 26th "P" Company Special R.E. arrived in the trenches armed with 4 in. Stokes gas shells and at night they put over one thousand in eight minutes round Fosse 8. The enemy made no reply. "P" Company were satisfied and departed.

On September 9th Captain A. S. Neale, the adjutant, left the battalion and went to brigade as a staff learner. His services to the battalion had been great. He joined as a private soldier on mobilisation, was quickly promoted sergeant, went overseas with the battalion and was the idol of his platoon. He then went to England for a commission and joined the battalion after the Hohenzollern battle in 1915. He was soon made adjutant and served in that capacity for nearly two years with great efficiency. His example of cheerfulness, willingness, and good comradeship was unequalled. Captain H. R. Pochin took his place as adjutant.

CHAPTER XXXII

ST. ELIE

On the night of the 3rd/4th October the 4th relieved the 5th Battalion in St. Elie left subsector. They had been in divisional reserve at Fouquieres and "A" and "B" Companies had been training for a raid. At 10 p.m. on October 6th under Lieutenant G. L. Lea "A" and "B" Companies raided the enemy line. They were preceded by an eighteen-pounder barrage. The operation had been carefully worked out behind the lines, and for once no hitch occurred and everything went according to plan. The party penetrated the enemy's second line but found it empty. Dug-outs and machine-gun emplacements were destroyed with ammonal. Second-Lieutenant C. F. Saunders took over the leading wave, Second-Lieutenant G. B. Taylor took over the second. Our casualties were one killed and four wounded. The enemy retaliation was not heavy. That was the kind of night life that went on at St. Elie. It was a very good evening's entertainment for those who liked that sort of thing. The whole operation was well managed. Lea had had much experience of raids, he knew all the tricks of the trade, and most of the snags and how to avoid them. The men knew the job too ; they could destroy a dug-out or wreck an emplacement almost as easily as they could open a tin of bully beef. The artillery were also most efficient ; they timed the barrage to a nicety, and were not so fond of dropping a shell or two short as they had been in earlier days. Raiding had become a fine art, and in this instance "A" and "B" Companies obtained full marks.

The Boche would try his hand at raiding also. And on October 16th at 4.50 a.m. the enemy attempted a silent raid on one of our Border Crater posts. He was driven off leaving a wounded man in front of our wire. Second-Lieutenant J. H. Watson and No. 200500 Sergeant Worth fetched him in at a considerable risk to themselves. Another brave deed in the interest of humanity.

About the same time a Hun walked up to our Farmer's Lane post and when challenged surrendered quite cheerfully. He gave a lot of useful information and stated that his division was being relieved on October 18th. On the night of the 18th our batteries plastered all the enemy tracks behind their line hoping to catch them in close order during relief.

On November 15th the battalion left the St. Elie Sector and went into draughty huts at Mazingarbe. On the 21st they relieved the 5th Battalion in the front line at Hill 70. It was a filthy kind of sector; apologies for trenches, shell holes, equipment, bodies, dud shells and all the inglorious panoply of war littered the place. Luckily, the so-called trenches were on the top of a hill and observation towards the enemy was good and the approaches in rear of the trenches were invisible from the enemy's lines.

The 5th had worked hard at the new sector and had had a quiet time. The 4th had only been in the trenches twenty-four hours when the enemy put down a hurricane bombardment at 6 a.m. using shells of every calibre. Under cover of this they rushed one of our Lewis gun posts and killed or wounded every man in it. Our artillery and machine-guns put down a heavy barrage on the enemy front line and knocked hell out of the returning raiding party. Our casualties were one missing, three killed and twenty-two wounded. The rest of the day was quiet. The Tigers were licking their wounds. So much for Hill 70.

On November 26th the battalion handed over to the 6th Yorks. and Lancs. and went into huts at Noeux les Mines.

CHAPTER XXXIII

CAMBRIN RIGHT SECTOR

ON December 1st the 138th Brigade were ordered to leave Noeux les Mines to take over the Cambrin Sector which was just north of the St. Elie Sector. Everybody was rather pleased as the G.O.C.'s inspection due for December 2nd was cancelled.

So the battalion moved to Annequin to support billets where they were employed in working parties and carrying fatigues. Lieutenant-Colonel T. P. Fielding-Johnson arrived from the 4th Lincolns and took over command from Lieutenant-Colonel G. R. A. Beckett.

The enemy did not make the battalion very welcome in its new quarters but assiduously bombed the back areas and dropped several bombs in Sailly Labourse, the transport H.Q. Four transport drivers were wounded but luckily the Q.M.'s stores and transport lines escaped.

At 8.30 a.m. on the 8th the battalion moved from billets at Annequin and marched up to the trenches to relieve the 5th battalion. The relief was complete by 11.15 a.m. The ground allowed the relief to be carried out by day which was a much more gentlemanly way of doing things than crawling up at night by stealth, tripping over wires and falling into shell holes. Troops are much more full of fight when they are full of breakfast. The trenches taken over in the Cambrin sector were those from which the 46th Division had attacked with so much élan on October 13th, 1915. They were now vastly improved and there were many tunnels and deep dug-outs. Altogether the Hohenzollern Redoubt was a much healtheir spot than it had been two years before.

However, the Boche started to liven things up the day after the 4th Leicesters arrived. At tea-time they put down a heavy barrage of trench mortar shells of all sizes on the front and support lines. The Leicesters were not going to stand this so they rang up the Canadian Field Artillery who promptly dropped a suitable barrage on the enemy's line. Lieutenant Jackson, holding the left sector of the front line, "reported that he thought he was being raided" (War Diary) so our Lewis guns opened enfilade fire to the left and artillery converged their fire on the threatened spot, Mad Point. At about 6.15 p.m. the enemy fire died down without his infantry having effected an entry into our trenches. That is a fair sample of everyday trench life. Trench mortar shells exploding in all directions. Artillery support in the twinkling of an eye. Murderous enfilade fire by machine-guns. Preparations to withstand the enemy's attack to the last gasp. Messages to brigade to have reinforcements ready. Thousands of pounds worth of projectiles flying through the air. Hundreds of soldiers armed to the teeth, ears and eyes in box respirators, still "full of strange oaths" but now nicely clean shaven! And what is the result? "Our casualties one man wounded." We have no record of the enemy losses during that tempestuous tea-time interlude but we hope . . .

Two days later at 1 a.m. the enemy put over two hundred gas shells. The alarm was promptly given and respirators were so quickly donned that only one man was slightly gassed. A dud shell was dug up behind the reserve line, sent to Army H.Q. for examination, and found to contain phosgene.

In the afternoon the 5th Sherwoods on the battalion's right raided the enemy's third line and brought back five prisoners. A dummy barrage and smoke screen was put down on each flank just before the raid which successfully diverted the enemy's fire from the raided spot. Raiding was not now a haphazard affair, but a carefully worked-out business proposition, efficiently supported by the troops on the flanks and by artillery who had unlimited ammunition.

Next day, December 12th, the enemy were again busy with their trench mortars, their idea being to blow in the tunnels which were being used as communication trenches. At 8.30 p.m. we projected gas on to Fosse 8 and covered our front with a heavy bombardment. A gas officer from the American Army came up to see the fun. He probably saw more than he bargained for, because at 10 p.m. the enemy opened a heavy bombardment with artillery and T.M.'s. Entrances to tunnels and galleries were smashed, the telephone wires were cut and communication broke down for some time. The enemy plastered the back area with mustard gas, and respirators were worn at battalion H.Q. for two hours, which was most annoying. It is difficult to check and sign returns in a box respirator even for the most efficient of adjutants, and brigade do like to have their returns sent in to time. It looked as though the enemy were going to attack on a three battalion front so the three battalions in question sent up the "attack" signal. Then our guns let them have it, shrapnel, H.E., gas shells. That cooled the Boche ardour for the time being. But at 3.30 a.m. they again bombarded our front line with such intensity that communication broke down and up went the S.O.S. Our guns were waiting for it and down crashed the protecting barrage once more. The enemy who had been seen in No Man's Land disappeared; no one penetrated our trenches. By 4.15 a.m. everything was quiet. And Atkins was smoking a cigarette and murmuring with no apologies to Mr. Kipling, "The guns, thank God, the guns." In due course the

American gas officer left the trenches for less dangerous terrain realising that there were even warmer places than Salt Lake City.

Throughout the bombardment the 170th Tunnelling Company had behaved splendidly, sparing no effort to keep the tunnels open. "A" Company of the 1st Monmouth (Pioneer) Battalion was sent up and helped to put the battered trenches to rights. The Monmouths could dig. Our casualties were one killed and three wounded. We were lucky.

Next day (December 14th) the 5th Battalion relieved the 4th who went to billets at Beuvry in divisional reserve. The next five days were spent in cleaning up, resting and listening to martial music played by the drums who spent their time with the Divisional Depot Battalion while the 4th Battalion were in the trenches. The time passed quickly enough, the weather was cold and frosty, and on the 19th the battalion football team beat the Springboks (Divisional Supply Column) 2-0. Life behind the lines got better and better in some respects. Earlier in the war there had been few comforts for troops resting; now there were regimental canteens and Y.M.C.A.'s, football and bands. But if there was music in the air there were also more enemy aeroplanes coming over and dropping bombs at awkward moments in places where they were not required. On the morning of December 20th the battalion marched up to the trenches in a thick fog and relieved the 5th. The 5th had had an unexciting tour as the enemy had been quiet and good. The 5th had taken advantage of this inactivity and had worked like blacks putting the trenches and tunnels to rights; even the 4th, who were always critical of other people's work, were well satisfied when they found comfortable dug-outs where they had left a bed made of lousy sand-bags and a candle stuck in a bottle, and habitable trenches where they had left heaps of debris.

At 11.10 p.m. on the 21st Second-Lieutenant H. Markham took out a patrol of seven men to try to rush one of the enemy's posts. The party unfortunately came upon the post earlier than expected and was met with bombs and rifle shots. They, however, threw all their bombs into the post and, Markham having been shot through the foot, the patrol withdrew in good order— with the exception of one private soldier who asserted that they were returning in the wrong direction. He broke away from the patrol and ran towards the enemy's lines. A search was made for him later without success. All identifications had been removed from him before the patrol left our lines.

"The best way of instilling rigid discipline is close order drill," remarked the C.O. to the adjutant that night. "See that the battalion gets plenty of it next time they are out of the trenches." "Very good, sir," replied the adjutant with a knowing look at the R.S.M.

Christmas Eve came. The battalion was still in the trenches. Perhaps some thoughtful subaltern turned the tattered pages of a khaki pocket Bible and read of wise men of the East bringing presents of gold and frankincense, when suddenly the guns of men of the West belched forth iron and gas. Back went the Bible to the breast pocket; out came the box respirator. On the left the 42nd Division plastered the Huns with gas and H.E. at 6.30 p.m. On the right the Sherwood Forester Brigade projected gas at 9 p.m. That would give the Boches something to put into their Christmas stockings and make them think Santa Claus was giving red-hot pokers for Christmas instead of toffee apples. But the old Boche, who is nothing if not a humorist, though sometimes a grim one, turned his attention not to the right or the left but showered 77 and 105 m.m. shells on the H.Q. of the 4th Leicesters in such profusion that the C.O. and the adjutant felt aggrieved and confessed themselves surprised that there should be such churlish fellows in Christendom.

Christmas Day was quiet. The enemy did not seem to be trying. Snow fell during the afternoon and reverently spread a white sheet over all the poor broken bodies in No Man's Land. No attempt was made by the enemy to fraternise. Perhaps they knew that our gunners had carefully arranged a very heavy reception should there be any indications of peace and goodwill. So the last Christmas of the Great War for civilisation slipped by. Santa Claus could not understand it. The laughter of happy children of all nations was ringing in his ears : British, French, German, Austrian. "These men must have gone mad," he shouted as he whipped up his reindeer across No Man's Land. "They have, and aren't they making a bloody mess of things?" called back Gabriel as he dressed the ranks of the Heavenly Host for the Christmas Day parade.

CHAPTER XXXIV

1918 ARRIVES

THE old year went out on the battalion in brigade support at Annequin. The C.O., Lieutenant-Colonel T. P. Fielding-Johnson, felt very happy as he had a pass in his pocket for fourteen days' leave to U.K. U.K. was a good place. Major G. R. A. Beckett took over command and on New Year's morning marched the battalion up to the trenches. The weather was cold and frosty and snow was still on the ground. The enemy hotted things up with T.M.'s and artillery and on January 2nd at 9.20 p.m. attempted raids at three places on the brigade front, but they had no luck, and went back to their trenches feeling they had been wasting their time, and doubtless reported to their commander three miles behind that the British lines were impregnable and strongly held. Major Beckett and Captain Nugee were each awarded the Military Cross early in the month. As a sign of the times an officer of the U.S.A. Army, Captain Bowden, was attached to the battalion in the trenches for instruction.

On January 7th the 5th relieved the 4th who went back to Beuvry to divisional reserve. The next day was spent getting clean and ready for the long-delayed Christmas dinner. On January 9th at 9.45 a.m., in order to give piquancy to the feast, the brigadier looked over the battalion who were practising for the Army Commander's coming inspection. But if the brigadier looked stern and complained of a lack of spotlessness in the equipment and snap in the rifle exercises, Atkins looked respectful but was exceedingly joyful of heart. And why? Because shortly the beer would be on the table, and at 5 p.m., lo and behold, it was there accompanied by roast pork, brussels sprouts and potatoes, followed by plum pudding, rum sauce and oranges and apples. It was a great spread; it was a great night. The brigadier, General F. Rowley, and the G.O.C. Division, General W. Thwaites, visited all the companies. This time they were all smiles.

Next day training was much hampered by snow but it did not hamper the sergeants holding their Christmas dinner at Dou Dou Camp at 5 p.m. followed by a "smoker" which the officers attended. Sergeants' Mess Smokers are always good. This one was especially good as they collected eight hundred francs for St. Dunstan's Hostel.

The weather was very cold and there was more snow on the 13th when the battalion went back into the front line. The next day the thaw set in and it began to rain and the trenches began to fall in. This was rather awkward. The communication trenches became impassable. Every available man was put on to keep the trenches open. The 11th Division were coming to take over the sector in a few days and there was a fear that relief would be postponed if the trenches were in a bad condition. The work went on feverishly; the trenches continued to fall in. The relief by the 11th Division was postponed, and the 5th had to relieve over the top instead of using the communication trenches. Luckily the Boche was in a similar plight and there was little firing.

On the 19th the 4th were relieved by the 6th Yorks. and Lancs. and marched to billets at the tobacco factory at Bethune. Next day they marched five miles north-west to Mt. Bernenchon. Although Bethune was five miles from the front line they marched through it by platoons owing to danger from long range guns. Once through the town they marched by companies at one hundred yards' interval. The G.O.C. watched the battalion march by. He seemed pleased with the turn-out. He knew what a rough time it had just had in the line.

At this time the powers that be began to realise that the Spring would bring a great German offensive. The enemy had been able to reinforce their western front with troops from the eastern front owing to the Russian collapse. The British forces were sadly depleted owing to the expensive offensives they had conducted at Passchendaele and on the Somme. It was known the Germans would make a determined effort to break through before enough American troops arrived to enable the Allies to take the offensive once more. Therefore strong lines of defence were being constructed well in rear of the British front line.

The 4th battalion was ordered to carry out wiring under R.E. supervision on the Brown Line in the neighbourhood of Oblinghem near Bethune. Work was carried on spasmodically, as often there was a lack of required materials, principally barbed wire. A certain amount of training was carried on, and some days were spent in unloading barges on the canal.

From January 30th the 138th Brigade consisted of three battalions only, the 1/4th Lincolns being sent to the second line division. The 4th Leicesters received reinforcements from the 2/5th Leicesters. This system of reducing brigades from four to three battalions went on throughout the whole of the B.E.F. owing to the lack of personnel.

On February 2nd the battalion moved to the neighbouring village of Busnes. Here reorganisation and interior economy proceeded together with firing on the range. There was a good deal of wet weather but some days were bright and springlike.

On February 8th the brigade moved to Westrehem about ten miles south-west. From there the battalion moved next day to billets in Coyecque. A brigade tactical scheme was carried out during the move westwards and the battalion acted as vanguard to the brigade, and finished up by seizing ten crossings of the River Lys, and taking up an outpost line. It was a good day's work. The corps and divisional commanders had a look at the brigade as it marched out. They wanted to know what they had got in their crackers if it came to open fighting. At 5 p.m. the scheme ended and the battalion marched to billets in Coyecque. In two days' marching only one man had fallen out, which says a good deal for the feet and the guts of the battalion.

The battalion stayed at Coyecque from February 10th to March 1st. Everybody's energies were concentrated on platoon training in the shape of the Associated Rifle Association (A.R.A.) Competition. This competition included firing as a platoon, and advancing down the range with savage bayoneting of dummies on the way and opportune bursts of Lewis gun fire Fire discipline and control were severely tested. If there was going to be any open fighting the Higher Command were determined that junior ranks should know how to act on their own initiative. This is one of the instances when, after the passing of years, we stand up and take off our bowler hats to the supreme wisdom of the much criticised Higher Command. Doubtless they knew they were skating on very thin ice and that when the great German offensive came anything might happen. The Germans had already taught them that small groups of resolute men armed with machine-guns could play havoc with large detachments of infantry in close formation. They intended to profit by that lesson as the tuition had been expensive.

So life continued. It was now quite obviously a subaltern's war, that is, during training hours. Platoon vied against platoon in all the soldierly arts. Dummies made of sacks full of straw were made to look like Germans and savagely bayoneted, and concussed with the butt of the rifle. Special attention was drawn to the most vital parts of the body, and the rider was added that "four inches of bayonet would do the trick." Stranger oaths than ever entered the fertile brain of Willy Shakespeare were heard on the assault course. The Hun would shortly be at the gate but his progress down the garden path was not going to be unexciting.

The R.S.M. in addition to his other duties now conducted a riding class for officers. R.S.M. Robinson came from the regular cavalry. He knew all about the training of horses ; he knew all about the training of moustaches. He was a dapper little man and it greatly contented his soul to see his beloved horses circling round him once more. History does not relate what he said to the subalterns about their ragged seats, nor how ragged their seats felt when he had done with them. One can only imagine that he somewhat moderated the stock blasphemies of the cavalry riding master lest the innocent infantry susceptibilities should be shocked ; that he expatiated on the necessity of easing the hand and closing the legs on the command "Walk march" ; and that he rejoiced secretly when any unskilful officer parted company with his mount, simply because it reminded him of old times.

Second-Lieutenant W. L. Barber and No. 9 Platoon won the A.R.A. Competition in the battalion elimination and in due course competed unsuccessfully against No. 1 Platoon of the 5th Battalion, who eventually won the competition, beating platoons from the other two brigades of the division.

The battalion got a lot of football and the brigadier put up a cup for the best company team in the brigade.

Time was spent in innoculation, medical inspection, baths, lectures, gas drill, church parade, brigade tactical schemes, and the re-issue of steel helmets painted and marked with the battalion sign. The battalion was fit and hard as nails and on March 1st it left Coyecque and marched to Flechin and billeted there for the night. Next day the march eastwards was continued to Manqueville and the day following to Noeux-les-Mines. No man fell out on any of these days. The 4th Leicesters never had been much of a battalion for falling out, and they kept up their reputation.

CHAPTER XXXV

CAMBRIN SECTOR

NOEUX-LES-MINES was just behind the front line and on March 4th the battalion relieved the 9th West Yorks in the trenches in the Cambrin South Sector.

Everybody appeared to be happy now they were in the line again. Behind the line, however, things were different. Defences of all kinds were being constructed at a feverish pace. The Big Push was coming at any moment. The front line was expected to be wiped out and reliance was being put in heavily fortified positions in rear.

In the meantime the usual trench routine went on. Things in the front line were quiet. The battalion moved out to brigade support at Sailly Labourse and Annequin on March 8th.

The peace of Annequin was shattered next afternoon by a hail of 4.2's and 5.9's. One fell in the yard of the orderly room. One was enough; the orderly room moved.

The days of rest were spent providing working parties on reserve lines and strong points so that all might be ready when the Hun came. Atkins was getting rather tired of all this preparation and "wind." If the Boche was coming then the sooner the better.

By the 13th the battalion was in the front line again. On this day Second-Lieutenant F. W. Hussey took out a daylight patrol and twenty yards from the enemy wire he found a Lewis gun wrapped in a waterproof sheet and in good condition. Apparently this gun had been captured in a hostile raid but dropped in No Man's Land on the way back. Beside the gun lay a dead German; doubtless a brave man whose triumph had been short lived. The battalion were delighted with their find.

On March 20th, after a few days rest in divisional reserve at Beuvry, the battalion relieved the 5th Leicestershires in the front line near the Hohenzollern Redoubt.

March 21st, the day of the great German attack on the 5th Army, was peaceful in the Cambrin Sector except for heavy enemy gas shelling of our batteries. Next morning at 12.20 a.m. things began to liven up. The enemy dropped a heavy T.M. and artillery barrage on the sector and the sectors to the right and left. All communications went down almost immediately except those to the centre company commander who reported no infantry attack on his front. Meanwhile our guns had nobly responded to the call for assistance. Our guns at this period were always ready to belch forth salvoes of H.E., shrapnel, and gas. There were big guns and plenty of them ; they had plenty of ammunition and plenty of experienced gunners to fire it. This was 1918, not 1914 and '15, when a well-worn eighteen-pounder might only spit three rounds of shrapnel a day.

It afterwards transpired that the enemy had tried to attack our left company line but had been repulsed with rifle and Lewis gun fire. The main attack captured the front line trenches of the 8th Sherwoods and entered their reserve line from whence the enemy began bombing down our reserve line. He did not get far, however, and was soon heavily repulsed. Nine Boches lay dead in No Man's Land and two remained prisoners, and from them valuable identification was obtained. Our casualties were eight wounded and two missing. Where the two missing went no one knows. Perhaps the wily old Hun had obtained his object after all.

The remainder of the tour was quiet and on the 24th the 5th Battalion relieved the 4th who went back to Sailly.

The 4th had not long reached Sailly when a very strong "breeze" blew up from brigade. One of the prisoners captured by us on the 22nd was causing a lot of trouble and inconvenience. He stated most emphatically that an enemy attack with three divisions was to take place on the 25th between Hill 70 and the La Bassee canal. This confirmed reports that had been received from our ground and air observers. Disconcerting news of the Boche attack in the south was beginning to trickle through and everyone except Private Atkins was beginning to wear a worried look. The higher the rank the deeper the gloom.

So instead of bathing themselves and writing home as behoved troops in rest, battalion H.Q. and "A" and "B" Companies spent their time marching and counter-marching to the Noyelles-Grenay reserve line, so that they might be ready to sell their lives expensively when the Hun attacked. But the Hun did not attack. This infuriated Atkins ; he dilated at length on the folly of taking prisoners ; he stated with great heat that no Boche was a good Boche till he was a dead Boche. He made assertions about the ancestry of this particular Boche prisoner which, though interesting from an anthropological standpoint, were quite unprintable.

The staff, with a little knowledge of what was happening further south, issued order and counter-order with tightened lips. Atkins, with no knowledge at all except an innate contempt for foreigners which had come down by easy stages from Crecy and Agincourt, via Waterloo, to his own particular little fire bay, sat picking his teeth, fondling his rifle, and muttering, "Let 'em all come."

CHAPTER XXXVI

THE WIND OF MARCH

MARCH is often a windy month, and this year with the Hun through the gate in many parts of the line, and with divisions crumpled and obliterated by the gigantic Hun attack, it is not surprising that in the portion of the line that held firm there were many anxious moments. In fact, no one was sure what would happen next. The real seriousness of the position was emphasised by Sir Douglas Haig's "Backs to the wall" order, and all ranks began to realise that the Allies were once more hanging on by their eyebrows. But Atkins knew that British eyebrows have ever been able to stand any strain; therefore he was unperturbed.

On March 26th there was talk of the division moving south to where the battle was raging, but next day orders were altered and the brigade was allotted to the Hill 70 Sector, north of Lens. At dusk the battalion moved out of Sailly Labourse to Les Brebis. Next evening at 10.20 p.m. the battalion relieved the Fiftieth Canadian Battalion in the trenches of Hill 70 Left Sector, which had been held by the 5th Leicesters the previous November. The relief was quiet, but it was a soaking wet night. Some days the enemy was uncomfortably quiet, which generally meant that he was preparing something uncommonly unpleasant. At 4 a.m. on March 30th an enterprising enemy patrol attempted to bomb one of our advanced posts, but was driven off by rifle fire. Everyone kept very much on the alert as the Hun was definitely on the war path. His aircraft showed increasing activity, and the sounds of battle still rumbled away to the south.

On April 2nd at 8 a.m. a battalion of the Sherwood Foresters of the 11th Division, who were on our left, carried out a raid on the enemy's line under cover of a smoke screen. Our left support company saw a party of Germans trying to enfilade the raiders from the south with a light machine-gun, and our men promptly frustrated their efforts with rifle and Lewis gun fire. The Boches were annoyed and rained 77 m.m. shells on our support and communication trenches. By 10 a.m. the show was over and all was quiet for the rest of the day.

Next evening at dusk Second-Lieutenant F. W. Hussey took a patrol into No Man's Land, and thirty yards from the enemy wire he discovered a concrete pill-box inside which was a vertical shaft apparently communicating by a tunnel with the German front line. Hussey was intelligent; he was also extremely energetic. Back he went and reported his discovery to his company commander and asked for the wherewithal to destroy this sink of iniquity. Two nights later Hussey was again in No Man's Land; once more he stealthily approached the pill-box, but he and his patrol were not as stealthy as they might have been and the enemy opened a brisk rifle and machine-gun fire. This did not deter Hussey and his men though it must have been decidedly unpleasant as they were carrying twenty pounds of ammonal. However, they successfully lowered this charge on a wire down the shaft and blew it up. Then they went away contented with bullets whistling round their trouser legs.

A day or two later the battalion was badly shelled while in brigade support and gas masks were worn from 5 a.m. till 1 p.m. as there was no wind to blow the gas away. Luckily some of the dug-outs were gas-proof, but twenty men went to hospital, and almost everyone in the battalion was more or less affected as the gas continued to hang about in patches for many hours after.

On the 12th, after over a fortnight in the front and support line, the 4th Leicesters were relieved by the 1st Canadian Mounted Rifles and marched out to Sains-en-Gohelle, from which they marched to huts at Hersin where they rested but were under orders to move at four hours' notice. They remained at Hersin for ten days. Sometimes they were under orders to move at four hours' notice. Sometimes at one hour's notice. The battle still hung in the balance; anything might happen at any time. Living on a volcano behind the line was almost as trying as living on a mine in the line.

The time was not wasted. The men bathed and became clean in the baths at Barlin. They went through a gas chamber for practice. They trained for open warfare, and the section commanders became even more important than before. They practised field firing to the annoyance of those remaining villagers who would have tilled the soil over which they fired ball ammuni-tion. "What a waste of their time and ours," cried the French peasants whose farms they defended. "But then the English were always mad."

During this period a large number of men went to hospital with a complaint that might have been influenza or might have been caused by gas. The illness generally lasted about four days and was accompanied by a high temperature. The 5th Battalion had it even worse than the 4th.

On April 24th orders were received to move to Division. The battalion marched via Barlin and Houdain and arrived in billets at 4.30 p.m. Next evening the battalion moved north to Fou-quieres where the brigade formed the divisional reserve, the other two brigades being in the line.

Fouquieres was a small village just south of Bethune. It might have been a pleasant place in times of peace, but it was distinctly unhealthy now. The German gunners persistently dropped 5.9 shells into the parish, and on the 26th one hit a tree near the camp of the 4th Leicesters and killed one man and wounded eleven others.

The brigade went into the line on the 28th, the 4th Battalion being in brigade support at Essars relieving the 5th Sherwoods. Battalion H.Q. was in a house at Essars and the rest of the battalion were scattered in breast works and shelters. Life was very primitive. Essars was shelled continuously, and for some reason the enemy shelled the church with great regularity.

At 1 a.m. on May 3rd the battalion relieved the 5th Lincolns in the front line. What a front line it was! Isolated shelters and shell holes. Nothing that made for either security or comfort. However, the 4th Leicesters got their coats off to the job. No movement was possible by day, but at night large patrols went out, and under their cover working parties connected up the shell holes and shelters with trenches, and put out wire in front of them. It was a hard life. Little rest and lots of shelling. No Man's Land was the scene of many skirmishes with hostile patrols, and the enemy had a habit of opening fire with machine-guns from unexpected quarters. Enemy aircraft persistently patrolled the front, and any movement by day brought down hostile artillery fire. Casualties were frequent, but nightly the line was strengthened quietly by stealth and sweat.

No one in the 4th Battalion wept when the 5th South Staffords relieved on the night of May 6th. The battalion marched to Vaudricourt to bivouac; they were shelled on the way out and had four men hit. An unpleasant incident; a medley of blood, moonlight, and groans.

Rest at Vaudricourt was not a time for idleness. The battalion bathed and clothing and boots were repaired. The M.O. held an inspection; so did the Armourer-Sergeant. The C.O. inspected one platoon per company and the Padre held a church parade.

The atmosphere was unquiet; an attack was expected on the morning of May 10th. The brigade was placed in divisional reserve, and on the 9th took up positions near Bethune, north of the Beuvry-Bethune road. However, the old Boche did not attack and nothing happened but a slight bombardment of gas shells, and the battalion returned to Vaudricourt. On the evening of the 10th the battalion was once more on its way to the front line.

For a week there was comparative quiet in the line, but on May 17th the enemy bombarded Battalion H.Q. at Gorre Chateau continuously all day with gas shells. Towards evening the intensity of the bombardment increased. It was not easy to find out how those at Battalion H.Q. were faring. Captain A. B.

Pick in command of "A" Company in reserve did not like the look of things, so he sent up some of his men to join "D" Company in support to be out of the shelling and to be more handy in case of attack.

At last the shelling died away, but the gas hung about and great care had to be exercised in approaching Battalion H.Q. The C.O., Lieutenant-Colonel T. P. Fielding-Johnson, the Adjutant, Intelligence Officer, Signal Officer, M.O., and thirty-four other ranks became casualties. In fact, all the officers at Battalion H.Q. were gassed, so Captain A. B. Pick came up from "A" Company and took over command of the battalion until the evening, when Major G. R. A. Beckett arrived from the Q.M. stores with Second-Lieutenant D. W. Howath to take over the respective duties of C.O. and adjutant. That night the battalion was relieved and went back to bivouac in Vaudricourt Wood. Next day more men were sent to hospital as the result of the gas. Others who had been in contact with gas were sent to the field ambulance to have their clothes disinfected in the Thresh disinfector. Gas is vile stuff in warfare ; better were it if its inventor had never been born, or had been neatly strangled at birth. Gas brought into warfare in 1915 a spirit of bitterness hitherto unknown in European armies. Gas brought into the bodies of men a bitterness that sometimes lingers in them still, and of which they will not be rid until they die. If you hear an old gentleman coughing and spitting and generally looking green about the gills after breakfast, pause before you pigeon-hole him as a debauched old roué, for he may only have been serving his country on the Western Front.

The rest of May was comparatively uneventful. The line was being strengthened all the time. There was a good deal of gas shelling by the enemy. Our trench mortars bombarded hostile posts, and the enemy T.M.'s replied suitably in due course. Every night wiring parties were working in No Man's Land, and they were covered by patrols who were continuously on the prowl.

The last day of the month found the battalion washing themselves behind the line at Vaudricourt in the warm sunshine, and as night fell Lieutenant-Colonel F. W. Foster, M.C., arrived and took over command of the battalion.

CHAPTER XXXVII

JUNE, 1918

VAUDRICOURT in June was not unpleasant. Men who sleep in bivouac in fine summer weather wake up fresh with the sun pouring down on the dewy grass. No headaches, no mouths like the bottom of a parrot cage. Vaudricourt Park was a pleasant place; it was a good bivouac; and the clerk of the weather was kind. Everything in the park was beautiful until the brass hats arrived. A Brigade Ceremonial Church Parade was ordered for Sunday, June 2nd, in Vaudricourt Park at 10 a.m. The G.O.C. would be present. Drill order with rifles and soft caps. This meant spending most of Saturday "sloping arms" and "fixing bayonets." However, the battalion bore the situation with fortitude. They listened to the service conducted by the Reverend R. K. Davis, M.A., and offered up little prayers that the eyes of the G.O.C. might be blind to any ragged "slopes" or clumsy salutes. The brigade band thumped out the hymns. The Lord's Prayer rumbled out of a thousand throats. The Padre with uplifted hand prayed for "the Peace of God which passeth all understanding." Then, headed by the drums playing the regimental march, the battalion in column of route marched past the G.O.C. There are worse ways of spending a Sunday morning.

Next day a draft of one hundred and eight other ranks arrived. They were duly paraded and posted to companies. The battalion could do with them. That night the battalion relieved the 6th South Staffords in the front line. They were shelled with gas on the Essars Road on the way up. Very pleasant for the new draft!

At this period a lot of work was done by night on the Liverpool line, which was the second and stronger line of defence. Endless energy was spent in wiring, revetting, and improving this trench, which had a stream with deep banks in front of it, greatly strengthening the position.

Life in the trenches was still quiet. Peaceful war was the order of the day, and strenuous work and patrolling the order of the night.

A "Sports and Horse Show" took place at Vaudricourt on June 14th. Everybody enjoyed themselves. The brigadier presented the prizes.

While resting, a platoon and all the signallers carried out a signalling practice with a contact aeroplane. The C.O. and adjutant watched and were duly edified. In the evening the battalion marched for an hour wearing box respirators. Were these signs of the times? Sports and horse shows. Brigade band playing selections in afternoons. Surely things were looking up. The Hun was not hammering at the gate so hard. Contact aeroplanes and marching in box respirators. Could these mean the possibility of an advance? Atkins pondered these things in his heart, swigged "ving blong," and became optimistic.

Flaming June passed. Another good June spoilt. There are never too many Junes in a man's life. It is the cheerless Novembers, the wet Februarys, and the bleak windy Marchs that seem to come too often. However, this was the last bloody June of the war. Atkins did not know it; he was quite resigned to the war going on for ever. Winston Churchill did not know it; he thought 1919 would be the year of victory. Foch did not know it. Haig grown optimistic thought perhaps it might just be on the cards. Ludendorff and Hindenburg dreaded what July might bring forth.

For the 4th Leicesters June and July, 1918, meant trenches at Gorre and Essars, and rest at Vaudricourt Park. Plenty of work, plenty of shelling, some casualties, and some rest.

July 8th was a busy day. The battalion formed part of the brigade guard of honour to the Corps Commander, who visited Gosnay and presented medals to R.Q.M.S. W. Robertson, Sergeant J. Watts and Lance-Corporal R. H. Pexton.

R.Q.M.S. W. Robertson had served many years in the Volunteer Battalion of the Leicestershire Regiment before it became the 4th Leicesters. He had served in the Leicestershire Volunteer Company in the South African War. He had served as R.Q.M.S. to the 4th Leicesters the whole of the time they had been in France. He was known to the rank and file of the battalion as "Old Robbo," who looked up to him with respect not unmingled with fear. He had a short sharp way of saying things. What he said was absolutely to the point. He did not suffer fools gladly; in fact, he did not suffer them at all; they did all the suffering. He had a complete understanding of the verbs "to scrounge," "to wangle," "to dish out," "to pack up." Sometimes he called a spade a spade; sometimes he had other names for that useful implement. He preferred Bass to Bock. His duties were concerned in clothing and feeding the battalion, and never through his fault was the battalion cold or hungry. The rations reached the line every night. There were blankets enough when the battalion was in rest. He did his duty with relentless efficiency. Therefore he was a man whom the King delighted to honour.

Sergeant J. Watts was Transport Sergeant. He was with the transport on mobilisation when it trotted up and down the New

Bedford Road at Luton tied up with string. He was there when the mules first arrived; he was there when they were embarked in the "City of Dunkirk." Since then he had ridden up the line night after night with rations and stores. Dirty nights at Kruisstraat. Dirty nights at Souchez. Dirty nights at Gommecourt. He knew them all. If there was trouble with broken-down limbers, or wounded mules, he was there to see that the show went on and the rations reached the dump. He looked after his transport like a good father looks after his family. The 4th Leicesters had several transport officers during the war and they all recognised the ability and devotion to duty of Sergeant Watts.

July was a quiet month in the trenches as quiet months go, but it had its high spots. On the night of July 21st/22nd a patrol under Lieutenant G. Cashmore succeeded in rushing an enemy post and obtaining an identification. A job needing judgment, dash, and guts, coupled with a good slice of luck.

On July 30th an identification was badly wanted by brigade in a hurry. So Corporal Ashton, full of fight, went into No Man's Land with a couple of privates; stalked an enemy post, shot the sentry; then shot up all the Boches of the post except one whom they compelled to surrender and to crawl back with them to our lines. A thoroughly brilliant and dashing piece of work. The motto of the 4th Leicesters was becoming :—"You want the best prisoners, we get them." The brigadier was delighted; he probably got a good mark from the Divisional Commander. Anyhow, Corporal Ashton got the D.C.M. and thoroughly deserved it. Exit July in a blaze of glory.

The fourth anniversary of the outbreak of war found the battalion in the trenches. Things kept pretty lively. There was a lot of patrolling in No Man's Land. The enemy was harassed at every opportunity.

The news of the British success at Amiens on August 8th soon came through and everybody became optimistic. The rumour factory went on overtime and the Boches were daily expected to retire, retreat in disorder or lay down their arms. Even closer touch was kept with the enemy by the patrols, and on August 20th the Boche was found to be retiring on the battalion front. Companies moved forward and established liaison posts with the division on the right. A further advance was made next day and a line of outposts was established. Open warfare had recommenced. On the night of the 23rd when relieved by the 5th Leicestershires the outpost line stretched from Le Touret in the north to the south-west of Rue de l'Epinette.

On the 26th, after two days in support, the battalion went back to rest at Fouquieres. The rest consisted principally in hard training for open warfare. The Boche was at last going back and he must be kept moving. On September 1st the battalion was in support at Gorre. On the 3rd the 46th Division in conjunction with the 19th Division attacked, took some ground and fifty prisoners. On the next day the line was still further advanced. On September 5th the battalion moved back to Fouquieres and carried out training for the next five days Everyone was fit and very full of fight. The rumour factory was still hard at it. Major-General W. Thwaites, C.B., had just handed over the division to Major-General G. F. Boyd, C.B., C.M.G., D.S.O., D.C.M. A D.S.O. and a D.C.M. was an unusual combination but one that appealed to Private Atkins, T. There would probably be less mucking about, though there might be more fighting. Having gained a D.C.M. himself, he might shower them more plentifully on the men of his division. "He must be some good or he would not command a division at his age," murmured the wise men in the ranks.

Major-General G. F. Boyd had a most attractive personality. He was young. He was handsome. He had gained a commission from the ranks, having won the D.C.M. in the South African War. He had a smile for everyone. He had a brain like lightning and an imagination as vivid. He had unbounded energy, he thought of everything, he forgot nothing. He had been lucky, he had been successful, and he intended to be still more lucky and successful. When the 46th Division (the division of Hubert Hamilton, Montagu Stuart-Wortley and William Thwaites) was placed in his hands he seized it as an expert swordsman seizes a priceless blade. He smiled. This was just the weapon he had been looking for. He would wield it as it had never been wielded before. He would breathe his luck upon it ; with it he would leap to victory. And he did.

J

CHAPTER XXXVIII

BEFORE BELLENGLISE

On September 11th the battalion left Fouquieres and marched to Chocques and entrained there at midnight. An hour later the train rumbled off in the darkness. The usual bumping and groaning over the French railway, through St. Pol, through Amiens, and at 3.15 p.m. next afternoon the battalion detrained at Mericourt l'Abbe and went into billets in semi-demolished buildings.

The surrounding country was a wilderness. It had been heavily fought over recently and the whole landscape had a derelict appearance. Few civilians were to be seen.

The 46th Division was now part of General Rawlinson's 4th Army. It was quite obvious that they had not been sent south for fun, but for fighting. Amid the scenes of destruction they began training hard for open warfare. They did field firing; they had field days. After three years' fighting they had little use for field days; if they must carry out attacks at great labour in open formation, then let them do it against a real enemy, so there would be fewer recriminations from the brass hats when the show was over. The division was not up to strength, but it was fit and it was spoiling for a fight. If there was open warfare then it was going to have its share. Anything to get out of the mouldy billets and tedious training of Mericourt.

On September 18th the battalion left Mericourt and marched to the sugar factory at Ribemont, where it embussed at 11.15 p.m. and went via Albert and Peronne to Estrees arriving at 5.30 a.m. It is not much fun spending the night on the top of a bus, especially if it is jolting over bad roads, groaning up inclines, and stopping now and then for apparently no reason whatever. Thus the convoy moved, and the bones of Atkins were weary and the seat of Atkins was sore when the end of the journey was reached. By 6.30 a.m. the battalion was in bivouac at Tertry, and for the remainder of the day it slumbered and slept.

Next day training was carried out, but it was quite obvious to everyone that there was very shortly going to be a bloody battle. Tertry was about a dozen miles from the Hindenburg Line, which was the Hun's most important bulwark. Once this was broken through anything might happen, but it was going to be a tough job, as the Hun was an excellent soldier behind a prepared position.

On the evening of the 20th an advance party of five officers and thirty-eight other ranks went up to the line. Next day at

2.30 p.m. the battalion followed and arrived in position west of Pike Wood at 9.30 p.m. They were badly bombed by hostile aeroplanes on the way up and had ten men hit. They realised that this was not going to be a field day.

The line taken over had been held by the 1st and 4th Australian Divisions. It consisted of captured German trenches, and had one great advantage; it overlooked the German position. The defences on the St. Quentin Canal, Bellenglise, and the villages of Nauroy and Levergies could be plainly seen. The Germans could not move without being observed. In fact, the tables of Ypres and Souchez were now turned; instead of the Boche holding the heights, we held them. Besides this we had superiority of fire and we had taken the offensive. No more was the Hun able to sit in comfort observing our lines and firing through telescopic sights every time he saw a head appear or smoke rising when Atkins boiled his tea. If anyone was going to get sand in his breakfast it was going to be the Hun this time.

The main defence of the Hindenburg Line was the St. Quentin Canal. It had steep banks, and was heavily wired; there were trenches and wire both to the east and west of this obstacle; and there was a tunnel leading underground from Bellenglise to the trenches on the east of the Canal. Altogether it was an immensely strong position and considered by the Boche to be impregnable.

To the 46th Division had been given the task of crossing the St. Quentin Canal and breaking the Hindenburg line. After over a year of defensive warfare the division was delighted with the chance of open fighting. It was not the question of taking a trench or two with terrific loss in order to straighten out a salient, but a decisive battle which, if successful, would lead to open warfare and victory.

September 22nd was quiet except for two enemy bombardments on our front line. The 30th American Division were on the battalion's left. They were very ready to fraternise with the 4th Leicesters. Their companies were about two hundred and forty strong; they were full of fight, reckless of casualties. They were on the fire-step all day, and they were generally hanging about when the battalion's rum was issued, having none of their own. They went out with the battalion's patrols armed to the teeth, and were sadly disappointed if the patrol returned without shedding blood. They were full of beans, but they lacked experience.

Next day there was rather more fire from the enemy; our casualties were one killed and six wounded. The time was spent improving the trenches and patrolling. Orders were received to send two officers and forty men to the 5th Leicesters who were to attack Pontruet, a village to the south-east, at dawn.

The 5th made the attack. They met with heavy resistance. Two of our trench mortars were unluckily knocked out almost at once. The fighting went on all day and into the night. Progress was made at first but most of the ground taken could not be held. Lieutenant J. C. Barrett of the 5th behaved with magnificent gallantry though severely wounded, and he was awarded the Victoria Cross. Lieutenant Hussey of the 4th Leicesters was killed. His party captured twelve prisoners. This action made the enemy realise that they were up against first-class troops, and there is no doubt that this sharp fighting shook the defence considerably though Pontruet remained in their hands.

CHAPTER XXXIX

NEXT day (September 25th) between 5 a.m. and 7 a.m. the enemy placed roughly one thousand shells of mixed calibre on our front; after this the day was comparatively quiet.

On September 26th the battalion was still in the line opposite Pike Wood and Peg Copse which were part of the German defences in front of the canal. Orders were received on this day from brigade to push forward and occupy any portion of the outpost system of the Hindenburg line that might be unoccupied. This sounded all right from the brigade standpoint, but when duly considered in the front line it boiled down to an unsupported attack on the enemy's line by the 4th Leicesters. This was rather more than the common sense of Colonel Foster could stand. So after a long "pow wow" with brigade the battalion was ordered to push forward strong fighting patrols to test the German defences.

Under cover of darkness Captain J. C. Ledward sent out a platoon of "B" Company in the direction of Peg Copse and Pike Wood—while Captain A. B. Pick of "A" Company sent out two platoons under Second-Lieutenant H. J. Partridge towards the enemy position south of Pike Wood.

Both parties found the positions occupied, the platoon opposite Pike Wood being heavily fired on by machine-guns, and some opposition was encountered by the party at Peg Copse. So the patrols withdrew.

Second-Lieutenant H. J. Partridge had crawled up to the enemy's wire; he had a piece chipped out of the butt of his revolver by a machine-gun bullet while lying out in a gap in the wire in front of his platoon. He was challenged by a German sentry in the wood and then fired on by two machine-guns. It was quite obvious to him that the position was strongly held and that if he led his men through the gap in the wire they would never return alive. So he lay still till the machine-gun bullets stopped kicking up the ground and cutting the wire round him, and then returned and reported that a battalion attack and a barrage would be necessary to capture the position.

The C.O. passed on this information to brigade. Brigade sent it to division. General Boyd knew that it was imperative that when the big attack was made on the Hindenburg line no strong resistance should be met on the west of the canal. He therefore gave orders for the 4th Leicesters to attack Pike Wood and Peg Copse next night, supported by the guns of an Australian field artillery brigade, who were to furnish a creeping and also a stationary barrage on the German trenches.

This was not a carefully prepared attack with every detail meticulously thought out beforehand, practised in the back areas, and dreamed about for nights previously by those concerned. It was quite an impromptu affair. At 4 p.m. on the 27th the 4th Leicesters were in the trenches waiting to be relieved with equipment all packed, lists of stores ready to be signed, and bosoms full of that pleasant optimism which is always present about the time of relief. Then at about 4.30 p.m. something startling happened. The C.O. appeared at "A" Company H.Q. waving a large map. The C.O. was not given to waving large maps at the time of relief. Obviously something dirty was going to happen. The cat was soon out of the bag. The battalion was to attack Peg Copse and Pike Wood at 7 p.m. preceded by a barrage. "A" Company on the right supported by "C." "B" Company on the left supported by "D."

Time was short, orders were only received at the last moment by some companies and things were so rushed that "B" Company had not time to reach the forming-up line in front of the trenches. However, Captain Ledward was equal to the occasion and advanced "B" Company from their trenches in time to be on "A" Company's left at the moment of attack. Three enemy aeroplanes came over just as the companies were forming up; they were flying very low but by the greatest piece of luck they went away without noticing the preparations for the attack.

It was a beautiful evening and the sun was setting as the battalion advanced. The German trenches were 700 yards distant but they were not parallel to the British line. As it was necessary that all the assaulting troops should arrive at the German line at the same time part of "A" Company had to be slowed up while the left platoon (No. 4) under Second-Lieutenant H. J. Partridge drew level as they had more ground to cross. Captain A. B. Pick commanding "A" Company did this in the proper parade ground style, blew his whistle, dressed the line, and then again signalled the advance. It was well done and showed the steadiness of the men.

Nos. 1, 2 and 3 Platoons of "A" Company reached their objective without a shot being fired at them. The barrage had kept the Germans in their deep dug-outs, and the attack took them completely by surprise. They surrendered freely without putting up much fight when our men reached their trenches and poked the noses of their Lewis guns into the dug-outs. No. 4 Platoon met with some resistance, and they killed quite a number of the enemy in hand-to-hand fighting, but Partridge and Sergeant Hemmings soon cleared the trench, and one German was so anxious to surrender that he flung his arms round Partridge's neck begging for mercy. Pick, who happened to come down the trench at this embarrassing moment, curtly asked his subaltern what he was "playing at." C.S.M. Adams of "A" Company entered one of the enemy dug-outs on the right of the line alone thinking that it was unoccupied. Unfortunately, it was full of Germans and he was killed and his body was not found until some days later. His entry must have given the alarm to the Germans because the company was soon being bombed from the right flank.

On the left "B" Company was equally successful. They reached their objective (Pike Wood) with only three casualties. Immediately the enemy realised what was happening they sent up a continual stream of S.O.S. rockets, but it did them no good. "B" and "A" Companies had the situation well in hand ; they quickly established communication with each other and captured two officers and one hundred and fifty men and sent them back as prisoners. At 7.45 p.m. up went the success rockets. "C" and "D" Companies were helping "A" and "B" to consolidate their position. Everything had gone according to plan. So far so good.

All that now remained was to hand over the fruits of victory to the two Stafford battalions of the 137th Brigade. It is difficult, however, to hand over the fruits of victory to someone who is not there, and the Staffords who were relieving were late and did not turn up till the early hours of September 28th. Thus a successful evening turned into a dirty night for the 4th Leicesters.

On arrival at Pike Wood "B" Company's flank was entirely in the air and open to enfilade fire from Peg Copse, so Captain J. C. Ledward took up a system of all-round defence with three platoons in front of Pike Wood and one in the wood itself. This position was intermittently attacked during the night and subjected to a persistent bombardment by trench mortars of small calibre. "D" Company had left one platoon with "B" Company in Pike Wood under Lieutenant T. R. Flynn, the remaining three platoons of "D" Company also left their bombs with "B" Company.

Shortly before midnight Captain Pick reported to Captain Ledward that the Boche were trying to outflank him on his right. Ledward immediately sent a platoon from "B" Company to help clear up the situation. The Germans were bombing up the trench on "A" Company's right and had to be held in check. Bombs were being slung all night. One unfortunate German N.C.O. was wounded on a traverse between the two opponents. There he lay groaning and shouting, while bombs burst all round him. Finally he became a prisoner, and was duly assisted to the dressing station, but he had spent a most unpleasant evening.

"A" and "B" Companies were now fighting completely on

their own and communications were practically non-existent. The enemy had now recovered from his surprise and was pushing up strong parties along trenches leading from the canal; all night long they tried to bomb their way back into their old position but without success. Lieutenant H. J. Partridge distinguished himself in maintaining a bombing block where he successfully held off the enemy for several hours. Lieutenant Wills, and his batman acting as his runner, did excellent work during the night in maintaining touch between the advanced platoons of "B" Company and repelling enemy attacks. Wills got the M.C. and his batman the M.M. for their heroic conduct.

Luckily the enemy did not shell the position as they were afraid of hitting their own men who were counter-attacking, but if it had not been for the extraordinary good show put up by the battalion the position would have been lost and would have had to be retaken in daylight, and this might have seriously hindered the subsequent operations.

At last, when dawn was breaking, the 5th and 6th North Staffords arrived (carrying ladders and wearing lifebelts from the leave boats) and relieved the weary companies, who retired to an area in rear near Ascension Farm.

Such was the Pike Wood fight. It was a battalion, almost a half-battalion show. "A" Company had lost heavily; their C.S.M. was killed and Second-Lieutenant Lacey was wounded. This action demonstrated afresh the fighting qualities of the battalion and the dash and initiative with which the junior ranks were imbued. The battalion had advanced 700 yards on a 500 yard front, taken one hundred and fifty prisoners, and with both flanks in the air held the position until relieved.

It was a bloody little fight of which any regiment might well be proud.

THE CANAL DE ST. QUENTIN NEAR BELLENGLISE.

THE CANAL DE ST. QUENTIN NEAR BELLENGLISE.

CHAPTER XL

THE BATTLE OF BELLENGLISE

IF the great Napoleon had been in Major-General Boyd's boots on September 29th, 1918, he could not have handled the 46th Division more successfully.

On September 28th the battalion received the following order while resting at Pingpost on Ascension Ridge :—

SECRET.

"At hour and date to be notified later 46th Division as part of larger operation will cross St. Quentin Canal, capture Hindenburg line and advance to Green Line."

"And the next thing, please," muttered the adjutant as he passed the missive over to the C.O.

The plan was for the 137th (the Staffordshire) Brigade to lead the attack, preceded by a tremendous barrage, and followed by the 139th (Notts and Derby) Brigade on the right and 138th (Lincoln and Leicester) Brigade on the left. When the Staffords had captured a line 1,000 yards east of the canal the 139th and 138th brigades were to pass through them and advance to the Green Line 2,500 yards east, and they in turn would dig in and be passed through by the 32nd Division.

It was a daring plan with tremendous possibilities. If it was successful it would mean a real break through and the smashing of the Hindenburg line.

Preparations went forward apace. New batteries appeared and quietly took up camouflaged positions till the back area was stiff with guns of all calibres. A continual stream of supply wagons congested all roads in rear. Ammunition dumps were carefully hidden in any place which offered cover. Over the whole proceeding the strictest secrecy was observed. The one thing that really mattered was surprise.

So at Zero hour, 5.50 a.m. on Sunday, September 29th, one of the heaviest barrages of the war crashed on the Hindenburg line. The Germans always said that the British never knew what a barrage was like as they were never under one of their own. One single gun gave the signal and then every Allied gun within miles belched. Dante's Inferno was a mere twitter to this. This was the real thing ; there were no two ways about it, this was quite definitely fiery bloody Hell. Hell let loose on earth. Hell with a capital H. Hell with the lid off. Heart-breaking, body-rending, shrieking, blasting HELL.

Just before zero hour Atkins caressingly fixed his bayonet, drank a libation of rum to the great god Luck, and chanted to that august deity the "Hymn before Action."

> "The bells of hell go ting-a-ling-a-ling
> For you and not for me.
> Oh, death where is thy sting-a-ling-a-ling,
> Or grave thy victory?"

Then as the barrage crashed the Stafford Brigade leapt from their trenches and advanced on the enemy, armed to the teeth and wearing lifebelts.

Following close on the barrage the Staffords captured the trenches west of the canal. Here the enemy put up a stout resistance, but the fog was thick, the barrage was sudden and the Staffords were not stopping for anything or anyone. On they went with reddened bayonets, leaving any remaining Germans to the tender mercies of the moppers-up. Down the canal bank they poured and crossed as best they could. In some places the canal was dry and the passage was easy; in others there was several feet of water, and lifebelts, life lines, and rafts were used. Some crossed by a concrete dam, some by Ricqueval Bridge which was captured in the nick of time as the enemy were about to blow it sky high. The fog still held, thickened by the smoke of the barrage. The machine-gun posts on the east of the canal were rushed and the teams bayoneted. The trenches near the canal bank were captured, and the enemy infantry, bewildered by the suddenness of the barrage and the fury of the attack, surrendered in hundreds; they put up but a poor fight. After checking to reorganise their men the Staffords swept on to their final objective 1,000 yards east of the canal which had been designated the Brown Line. Here they halted and consolidated the position. They were well up to time and had captured their objective in two hours and thirty minutes. The fog had been a godsend but it had made keeping direction difficult. They were superbly led. The gunners' shooting had been excellent. The Staffords had taken over two thousand prisoners. Their own losses were twenty-five officers and five hundred men. The Staffordshire Terrier is a fine fighting breed.

The 4th Leicesters spent the night of September 28th/29th on Ascension Ridge. In the darkness there was a continual coming and going; everywhere was congested. Guns, tanks, pontoons, ration parties, seemingly all jumbled together in the pouring rain. At 2 a.m. bombs, S.A.A. and water bottles were being issued. Two water bottles were supposed to be carried per man, a day's rations, and an iron ration. Overcoats were discarded and dumped in charge of two regimental police. Owing to the congestion the battalion could only draw ammunition, and neither water nor rations, but the battalion had been on active service for over three years and knew how to scrounge.

Before zero hour the 4th Leicesters were advancing through the fog, marching on compass bearings. They were badly shelled with gas crossing Ascension Valley. No. 4 Platoon lost twenty-two men out of twenty-six. Slowly but steadily the battalion pushed on in artillery formation, "B" Company leading. The role of "B" Company was to mop up behind the Stafford Brigade. This they did to some purpose, capturing many prisoners. The remaining companies passed through them and, following the Staffords' victorious advance, eventually found themselves on the Brown Line. By this time Colonel Foster and Captain Howarth, the adjutant, were casualties and Lieutenant Cashmore was mortally wounded. The command of the battalion devolved on Captain Lea who sent back to "B" Company (who were still mopping up west of the canal) for Captain Ledward. Before Ledward arrived Lea had launched the battalion on their final objective, the Yellow Line, which was about 1,000 yards in front of the Brown Line. There was little enemy resistance and by noon a report was sent to brigade that all objectives had been taken.

The fog lifted, the victorious Boyd rode on to the battlefield. Batteries rumbled over Ricqueval Bridge. R.E.'s, for once, perspired building pontoon bridges. Tanks crashed through unbroken wire. Germans surrendered in hundreds. Battalion H.Q. was established in a dug-out overlooking Springbok Valley. A F.A. Brigade came into action immediately on the left of this valley. The 30th American Division was attacking on this flank, and as the situation was uncertain the artillery brigadier asked "B" Company to push on to the high ground to the left and clear up the position. "B" Company advanced and made connection with the 8th Australian Division who were supporting and continuing the American attack.

During the consolidation of the Yellow Line "A" Company under Captain Pick were heavily shelled from the right flank and sustained some casualties.

The attack was subsequently carried on to the next objectives, the Dotted Blue and the Green Line, by the 5th Leicesters and 5th Lincolns. The enemy resistance now strengthened and his artillery activity increased but the rest of the day passed quietly, the only incident being the bringing down of an enemy aeroplane by Lewis gunfire on the battalion front. The 32nd Division passed through the battalion front during the afternoon.

Major G. R. A. Beckett, M.C., took over command of the battalion at 8 p.m. Captain Ledward took over the duties of adjutant.

The keynote of the Battle of Bellenglise is this : The battle was fought and won by the artillery. The concentration of artillery was probably the biggest in the history of the world. The guns stood wheel to wheel rank on rank as far as the eye could see. Walking back to brigade when they were registering was much more terrifying than the battle. The staff work on communications and supply was excellent, and the result was that at zero hour the heavens rained shells and the impregnable Hindenburg line made of ferro-concrete trenches was entirely and completely smashed. The behaviour of the infantry was magnificent, but without the guns they could never have obtained their objectives and held them even with the help of the fog. Besides smashing the German trenches the bombardment smashed the German morale. The human machine, like any other machine, breaks down when the strain becomes too great. Some of the German infantry had been unable to leave their deep dug-outs for forty eight hours owing to the bombardment, and the stench in the dug-outs was enough to make any German surrender.

That is a rough account of the battalion's part in the great attack; here are some of the details.

The battalion started off without its rations and without its rum. Two days' rations reached the battalion on the night of the 29th, but by then the battalion was sadly depleted by casualties.

On reaching the old British front line they found some rations left by the Staffords, so helped themselves.

Company officers visited brigade on the 28th to receive orders, but it was not until night that they received maps showing their objectives and operation orders. These orders had to be explained to platoon officers and sergeants by candle-light in any kind of shelter which could be found in a damp trench or bivouac.

The first duty of the battalion was to reach their old front line before crossing the canal. Their advance to this was held up by the Guards' machine-gun company who were firing an overhead barrage to aid the advancing Staffords.

It was about this time, when passing through our old support line, that the battalion received most of its casualties. They were heavily shelled and "A" Company lost a great many men; it was here that No. 4 platoon had a shell drop on each of its sections almost simultaneously, the men in many cases being literally blown to bits. It was here also that the colonel and adjutant became casualties. The adjutant, who was lying unattended, was very nearly ridden over by a gun team complete with gun. It was a most terrifying experience, but luckily he was noticed in the nick of time, and the gun swerved and missed

him. Second-Lieutenants Morbey and White were also wounded
west of the canal.

When the battalion reached their old front line they suffered
far less from shell fire. It was now quite daylight but a thick
fog of mist and smoke covered the battlefield. The advance
was continued across the same ground that the battalion had
passed over when attacking Pike Wood. On the battalion swept
or rather plodded, marching on compass bearings. At last they
reached the canal at a point where it was in a deep cutting. They
scrambled down the bank which was a mass of undergrowth
reinforced with barbed wire. Luckily one of the German plank
bridges remained and this was used ; the far end of it had been
destroyed but the water was only knee deep. Somehow or
other by various means the battalion crossed the canal and
climbed the bank on the far side. At the top of this "A" Company found the Staffords having a cup of tea with some German
prisoners. After a short session with the tea party "A" Company
noticed that the Staffords were becoming somewhat disturbed as
shadowy forms were seen advancing through the fog. Measures
were immediately taken to repel a desperate counter-attack.
The shadowy forms came nearer and became clearer ; fingers
toyed with triggers ; Lewis guns prepared to spit ; the canal was
not going to be sold cheaply. Then much to everyone's relief
the shadowy figures appeared to be perfectly good Germans
advancing with their hands above their heads as all good Germans
should. They had had enough of war and this loud Sabbath
had demonstrated unmistakably the advantages of discretion.
After the bombardment they had been through it is a wonder
that the poor fellows were not raving lunatics.

During the advance the obsession of all the company commanders and officers was to be on time. There was a time
stated at which each objective had to be captured, and the important thing was to be punctual. This was most difficult. The
fog hampered the advance, and made it difficult to find the way,
and the objectives which were easy to see marked in coloured
pencil on a map were extremely indistinct on the battlefield.
However, the battalion advanced and at the appointed time were
as near their final objective, the Yellow Line, as made no matter.
That they actually found their way to the objective through the
fog speaks volumes for their leaders.

"D" Company encountered gas in Ascension Valley and had
to put on gas masks. This company was lucky in finding a
wooden bridge across the canal still intact on a road called
Watling Street. They got somewhat lost in the fog after they
had crossed, but managed to collect one hundred prisoners.
They had to spread out at fifty yard intervals as they were short
of men and had a lot of ground to cover. They came under

machine-gun fire and the shells of one of our own guns which was firing short before they reached their objective—the Yellow Line.   Here they halted.   They were the left of the line and were not in touch with the American Division on their left—though an American officer and forty men suddenly appeared out of the blue and then disappeared almost as quickly.   "D" Company's left was on the road south of Etricourt and its right in the trench system by Knobkerry Ridge.   "D" Company proceeded to mop up this trench system under the guidance of Captain H. F. Papprill, and they sent back two hundred and fifty prisoners of various regiments.   Papprill had a slight altercation with a Prussian officer over a couple of epaulettes.   Papprill had developed the collector's mania for epaulettes and the German did not want to give his up.   As it happened to be Papprill's busy day words failed him for once, and he deftly turned the Prussian about and with one lusty kick in the pants landed him among his fellow prisoners.

At this moment things began to look black for O.C. "D" Company.   A German counter-attack was seen to be developing from the direction of Joncourt.   There was no sign of reinforcements from the 32nd Division and touch had been lost with the rest of the battalion.   Suddenly there was a clatter of wheels and a jingle of harness, and a field battery came galloping over the open ground, halted and unlimbered one hundred yards in rear of "D" Company.   Papprill was extremely gratified; the rank and file of "D" Company also evinced satisfaction.   It is pleasant to see a horse battery in full dress gallop round Olympia to the tune of "Bonnie Dundee" at the Royal Tournament.   It is exciting to see the same battery tearing down a Wiltshire lane in service dress on manoeuvres.   But to see a battery dash hell-for-leather across a bloody battlefield, unlimber, open fire at point-blank range, blow to hell a dangerous counter-attack and restore a doubtful fight—that is a sight for the gods (the gods of war, of course), a sight that military painters love to depict, a sight that brings balm to the harassed body and soul of Private Atkins, who shows his appreciation by muttering to his bosom friend two days later :—"Them guns come in very 'andy, Bill."

The Battle of Waterloo was fought on a Sunday ; so was the Battle of Bellenglise ; both were decisive, both bloody.

After nearly two thousand years of Christianity Christians have not the least compunction about slaughtering one another on the day they have dedicated to their Deity, the God of Love Perhaps, without wishing to appear unreasonably optimistic, we may venture to hope that in another two thousand years the hypocrisy of the people of Christendom will have decreased to

MAJOR-GENERAL G. F. BOYD, C.B., C.M.G., D.S.O., D.C.M., 46th (NORTH
MIDLAND) DIVISION (*left*); BRIGADIER-GENERAL J. V. CAMPBELL, V.C.,
C.M.G., D.S.O., 137th (STAFFORDSHIRE) INFANTRY BRIGADE (*right*); AND
OTHERS INSPECTING THE TEMPORARY MEMORIAL ERECTED TO THE FALLEN OF
THE DIVISION ON THE HIGH GROUND NEAR BELLENGLISE.

(*Reproduced by kind permission of the Proprietors of the Leicester Mercury.*)

such an extent that they will butcher one another on six days of the week only.

 . . . . . .

The late Field-Marshal Earl Haig, speaking at Leicester not long after the war, in referring to the deeds of the Leicestershire Regiment during the war, said :—"There is the outstanding exploit of the 46th Division in the breaking of the Hindenburg Line at Bellenglise to which I referred when I was last in this neighbourhood.   That attack, in which the one division took over 4,000 prisoners and 70 guns, formed one of the finest single actions of the whole advance, and Leicestershire battalions, the 4th and 5th, formed part of that division."

The names of the 4th Leicestershire Regiment's H.Q. and company commanders at the Battle of Bellenglise are as follow :—

BATTALION HEADQUARTERS.

Lieutenant-Colonel F. W. Foster, M.C.	Commanding
Major G. R. A. Beckett, M.C.	2nd in Command
Captain D. W. Howarth	Adjutant
2nd-Lieutenant W. L. Bass, M.C.	Intelligence Officer
2nd-Lieutenant A. F. Castle	Signal Officer
2nd-Lieutenant W. K. Fox	
Captain G. S. Brown, M.C.	Medical Officer
Lieutenant J. A. Tyler	Transport Officer
Lieutenant M. F. Shepherd, D.C.M.	Quartermaster
R.S.M. J. Holland	Regimental Sergeant-Major

COMPANY COMMANDERS

"A" Company—Captain	A. B. Pick
"B" „ — „	J. C. Ledward
"C" „ — „	G. L. Lea
"D" „ — „	H. F. Papprill

CHAPTER XLI

THE battalion spent the night of September 29th in some German dug-outs near their final objective. Rations came up about midnight, more than enough rations, more than enough rum. The battalion slept the sleep of exhaustion with full bellies. It was not a peaceful night; it was disturbed by frequent rumours of heavy counter-attacks, but no counter-attack came.

Next morning the eyes were gladdened by the sight of horse-men riding upon horses; this was unusual; horsemen had at other periods of the war been seen marching towards the line with a look of disgust on their faces and rifles in their hands, but that was only when the situation was critical and the P.B.I. were in sad straits. Now they appeared mounted, smiling, and armed with heavy swords. They raised the morale of everyone who saw them. Surely their presence meant a complete break through?

It transpired that their job was to take the Beaurevoir-Fonsomme line and keep the enemy on the move. But the Fonsomme line contained barbed wire and machine-guns, both bad for horse flesh, and before long the Greys returned and disappeared again on the west of the canal.

The battalion consolidated its position as best it could during the day and reorganised as far as possible. The casualties had been quite heavy enough and the fighting machine had to be patched up ready for the next encounter. Morale was very high; the sight of cavalry and German prisoners had done everybody good. But there was quite a lot of stuff flying about, and in certain quarters rumours of counter-attacks accompanied by wind.

Next day the battalion moved to Magny La Fosse and took over the left sector of defence from the 5th Leicesters. Battalion H.Q. was in gun pits in Fosse Wood, east of the village. Part of the battalion occupied cellars in the village; most of the buildings had been shelled to bits. There was an element of excitement in occupying one of these cellars, as anything might blow up at any time, for plenty of booby traps and mines had been left by the retreating Huns.

There was a good deal of shelling particularly of the forward companies, some casualties were caused by mustard gas shells, and Second-Lieutenant Brewis was evacuated suffering from extensive gas blisters.

The cavalry appeared again and it looked as though they might break through, but they were shelled and had to take cover in one of the valleys ; they formed far too good a target for the gunners.

There were several exciting air fights over Magny and one of our planes came down in flames close to the battalion. The bodies were so burned that they were quite unrecognisable.

On the 3rd of October the Battle of Ramicourt was fought. The division attacked on a two-and-a-half mile front, the Sherwood Brigade on the left, the Staffords on the right, the Lincoln and Leicester Brigade in reserve. The attack started at 6.5 a.m. in the dark behind a heavy barrage. The guns had been rushed up under almost superhuman difficulties. The objective was a line from Montbrehain on the north to Sequehart (exclusive) in the south. The northerly or left flank of the 46th Division would be in touch with the 2nd Australian Division, the 32nd Division were detailed to capture Sequehart on the 46th Division's right flank. So far so good, but in between the division and its objective was the Beaurevoir-Fonsomme line which was the enemy's last prepared position. If this was captured it might lead to a complete break through with the cavalry coming into their own. This line was only partially made and consisted of hastily dug rifle-pits, a line of shallow trenches supported every fifty yards by concrete shelters. The whole line was wired. Between this line and Montbrehain, the objective of the Sherwoods, stood the village of Ramicourt.

Zero hour was 6.5 a.m. There was a thick fog and a heavy barrage as the Sherwoods and Staffords began their advance. The fog soon cleared. The wire had not been cut as there had been no preliminary bombardment. The tanks supporting the two brigades made gaps in the wire and the troops poured through. The Boche put up a stout resistance, but the British meant business ; bayonets were soon bloody ; huddled lifeless bundles of field grey lying in the bottoms of the shallow trenches showed the fury of the assault. The Germans knew the importance of this position and they did their best to hold it. They put up a far tougher resistance than their comrades at Bellenglise.

The attack swept on and between the Fonsomme line and Ramicourt Lieutenant-Colonel B. W. Vann, V.C., M.C., commanding the 6th Sherwoods, was killed. Before the war Vann was curate at St. Barnabas Church in East Park Road, Leicester. At the outbreak of the war he laid aside his cassock and became a subaltern in the Sherwoods and went to France with the division in 1915. He soon distinguished himself in the trenches in front of Kemmel, and he got the reputation of being absolutely fearless and always being on the spot when there was any fighting. He was of magnificent physique, light-haired and with a strong handsome face. He was a brave man of the best type.

The Sherwoods captured Ramicourt and then Montbrehain. They could not hold the latter village and took up a line between the two villages on the Beaurevoir-Montbrehain railway with a flank position near Wiancourt.

The Staffords reached their objective, but they were badly shelled from Manniquin Hill and could only hold the lower slopes.

In fact, by about midday both brigades were pretty well fought to a standstill. They had both suffered heavy casualties and had met with considerable infantry and artillery opposition. The Sherwoods' right flank was in the air, not being in touch with the Staffords, and their left flank was thrown back at an angle. The Stafford position was not so far advanced as the Sherwoods. At this juncture the Lincoln and Leicester Brigade, who had been in support, began to take part in the battle.

On the morning of October 3rd two companies of the 4th Leicesters were in Magny La Fosse and H.Q. and two companies in the vicinity of Fosse Wood. During the morning the battalion was ordered forward in support of the Sherwood Brigade. It was an unpleasant advance. Batteries of our eighteen-pounders were in action and the effect of the violent discharge of these guns at close quarters was enough to raise the tin hat from the head. The ground sloped upward from Magny and at the top of the ridge the battalion came under enemy shell fire, but they plodded steadily on, taking cover as best they could in sunken roads. Second-Lieutenant Watson, who had just re-joined the battalion, was killed during this advance.

A message was brought by a tank to say that the Australians were held up near Wiancourt on the left and were short of ammunition. Not very heartening news. Battalion H.Q. was established in a railway cutting between Joncourt and Preselles, and while here wild rumours came through of a counter-attack coming from Sequehart. This was still more disquieting, as it seemed that the situation on both flanks was unsatisfactory. The amount of wounded coming down from the Sherwood Brigade kept Captain Brown, the M.O., very busy, and showed that things in front were none too rosy. However, it turned out that the alleged counter-attack was only German prisoners escaping from Sequehart, so the wind subsided and the battalion advanced to Swiss Cottage.

Once upon a time Swiss Cottage had been a pleasant little farm with a shady orchard, and the usual picturesque farm buildings of a French homestead. Now it was a shambles. The buildings were gaunt ruins, corpses lay in every direction, some of them crushed and mangled by tanks. Clothing and accoutrements littered the ground in profusion. The stench was foul. In this welter of filth and broken humanity Captain Brown established the Regimental Aid Post. Here he and his orderlies worked, patching up wounded, dosing them with morphia and sending them back as quickly as bearers became available. One small bright spot of mercy in an inferno of strife and inhumanity. It mattered not that shells burst overhead, that bullets spat with disconcerting frequency, that poison gas floated on the fetid air. The M.O. worked with fearless efficiency; the stretcher-bearers carried their pierced and bleeding burdens with dogged valour. Mercy and sacrifice had joined one another.

The orders of the 4th Leicesters were to support the Sherwoods and support them they did. They pushed on through Ramicourt and to the north and south of it. In this battered village they saw civilians who were now escaping to our lines after four years of German servitude. It must have been with a feeling of joy that they listened to the successful British bombardment at Bellenglise, but they became fearful as it came nearer and nearer, and when the shells began to drop in Ramicourt they were terrified. They did not know which way to move to escape destruction. In the middle of the main street lay the body of an old woman; beside her was a little hand-cart packed with the chattels which she was trying to save from her ruined home. After four wretched years her house, her hopes, and her life were shattered on the day of victory.

The Sherwoods who had advanced into Montbrehain were unable to hold this village against a heavy enemy counter-attack, and our troops were badly shelled from Manniquin Hill and Doon Hill. The 4th Leicesters were ordered to reinforce the Sherwoods. This meant advancing over open ground to reach a sunken road south of Ramicourt. They were in full view of the enemy and were heavily shelled by a high velocity gun firing at close range. A shell from this gun made a direct hit on a section and killed Second-Lieut. Mercer, who had joined the battalion only a few days before. The same shell knocked over Captain A. B. Pick and gave him a severe shaking, but fortunately he was able to carry on.

The sunken road when reached was found to be a most unpleasant place. A burnt-out tank adorned one of its banks. Men from a variety of regiments defended this position. Prisoners, wounded, signallers and machine-gunners were among the occupants of the road. The high velocity gun continued its attentions, enemy aircraft were unpleasantly active, but the object of greatest horror was a wounded German prisoner who walked up and down with half his face hanging down below his jaws. He looked such a terrifying spectacle that some suggested he should be shot and put out of his agony and thus cease to terrify those who looked his way. However, he was at length patched up and evacuated, but no one who saw him forgot his face.

The battalion then took up a position along the railway embankment between Ramicourt and Montbrehain and along a road covering Ramicourt on the north. This position was held throughout the night of October 3rd/4th and until the evening of the 4th when an Australian Pioneer Battalion relieved the 4th Leicesters.

The position on the railway bank was most uncomfortable. The bank was low and afforded scant cover. The night was extremely cold, shells from German and British guns arrived with unpleasant frequency, a large dump of German aerial torpedoes was close by and if a shell had hit them the balloon would have gone up with a vengeance. German counter-attacks kept sprouting from Montbrehain and had to be withered by Lewis gun fire. Ramicourt Station was like the slaughter-house of an atrociously untidy butcher, freshly killed Germans littered the platforms and rails ; one of the "dead" Germans came to life during the night and merciful "A" Company dressed his wounds and sent him towards safety.

In rear, but not in comfort, Battalion H.Q. was bombed by enemy aircraft who used parachute flares. There were no casualties, but there was little sleep. The company runners were the sole means of communication ; for them the age of miracles had not passed; in fact, they worked wonders daily and often twice nightly as well.

October 4th, 1918, was not a day that any member of the 4th Leicesters would like to live over again ; it was a case of hanging on by the eyebrows once more. The position of the Sherwood Brigade had been taken over by the Lincoln and Leicester Brigade. Efforts were made by "C" Company 4th Leicesters on the left of the line to get in touch with the Australians who were reported to be in Wiancourt but it was a hopeless task and the patrol who tried was shot to pieces by German machine-gun fire. The whole position was overlooked, shelled and enfiladed by the enemy on high ground to the east. At nightfall the battalion was relieved by the Australian Pioneers, and marched back to trenches round Etricourt. It was one of the most uncomfortable reliefs on record. The valley near Joncourt was full of gas, but as it was impossible to find the way in gas masks they had to be removed. The enemy aircraft kept dropping bombs and parachute flares. The battalion was a good target in this artificial light but luckily there were no casualties. The trenches when reached were most uncomfortable, supplies were scarce, and the troops spent a wretched night. Next morning the battalion moved west over the canal and rested in trenches which were formerly part of the Hindenburg line.

The Battle of Ramicourt was a great victory for the 46th Division; it broke the Beaurevoir-Fonsomme line, and if the cavalry had been up at the critical moment the fruits of victory might have been much greater. The Staffords had been held up on the slopes of Manniquin Hill, the Sherwoods had been unable to hold Montbrehain, and casualties in the division had been heavy and included five commanding officers. Two thousand prisoners had been captured and the way had been cleared for a further advance.

Ramicourt was a bloody battle; there had been much hand-to-hand fighting; the Boche had put up a stout resistance; he realised he was defending one of his last bulwarks. Many good men on both sides were slain. It was typical of modern open warfare; the sights were sickening, the noise appalling, and the discomfort intense.

CHAPTER XLII

THE battlefield of Bellenglise on the 7th of October presented a very different sight to the battalion than it had done on the day of the battle a week before. A miracle had happened. Where there had been battered trenches, shell holes of all sizes, wire entanglements and all the devastation of a modern battlefield there was now a huge armed camp. Tents, bivouacs, horse lines, gun parks, tanks, R.A.M.C. Everyone was pursuing his work with ruthless efficiency. The host was advancing, and must continue to advance. And after two days on the west of the canal spent in reorganisation the battalion moved eastward to Whistle Copse, and then on to relieve the 1st Buffs of the 6th Division in front of Fresnoy Le Grand, which was about eight miles from the battalion's starting point. The advance was not an easy one as much of it was made by night over broken country on a compass bearing. However, platoon and company commanders led their men well and by dawn on October 9th the battalion was holding the front line opposite Fresnoy, with Battalion H.Q. at Mericourt.

October 9th was a busy day. The battalion pushed patrols into Fresnoy, found it unoccupied by the enemy, but encountered some resistance from a railway cutting east of the village which the enemy was still holding. However, they were soon cleared out of the cutting and Fresnoy was freed from the German yoke.

The German yoke, according to the inhabitants of Fresnoy, had been extremely unpleasant. The civilians poured out to welcome the troops. Atkins began to feel heroic once more. It was a long time since he had been cheered by excited crowds in Leicester and Derby. Now after more than four years he was being cheered again in a remote little village in France. He felt gratified ; he hoped a quick hope that he might come through to the end of the war unscathed, as he quite realised that the end was not far off. But as this was his busy day he could not stop to air his French on the people of Fresnoy. The Boche was on the run, but he must be kept on the run.

So on the battalion went and after meeting with some gas and H.E. shells the line was occupied along the railway to the north-east of Fresnoy. Next day the battalion "leap-frogged" the 5th Lincolns who were holding the Bohain-Seboncourt Road and pushed on to a position south-west of Bois de Riqueval. Here they were relieved by the 5th South Staffords and 5th Leicesters. The battalion then marched back to billets at Fresnoy where Lieutenant-Colonel F. H. Edwards, M.C., 1st Bedfordshire Regiment, took command.

It was pleasant at Fresnoy. It was pleasant to be in civilisation once again. The town had been little damaged by bombardment, as only shrapnel had been used by the Allies. The billets were good, the inhabitants friendly, the weather just what autumn weather should be. Atkins was happy and contented. He bathed himself, got his shirt and pants washed by the young woman at his billet, brushed his clothes, polished his boots and attended Church Parade. It was obvious now that the war would soon be over. The townspeople of Fresnoy had no doubt about it. They had seen the British guns and transport passing through the town drawn by fat horses. They had seen the miserable German nags a day or two before ; the thing was quite obvious to them ; the army with the fat horses always wins.

Atkins enjoyed six happy days at Fresnoy. He had enjoyed the two days' fighting which had preceded the rest in billets. It had been open fighting in beautiful country little damaged by war. There were hedgerows and spinneys and sunken roads. It was interesting ; it was difficult to keep in touch with the troops on the flanks ; it needed good leadership on the part of platoon and section commanders ; but the sun shone, the grass was green, the russet tints of the trees were a sight that did the eyes good, and the Boche was on the run.

On October 16th the battalion was warned that they were to make an attack the next morning, and the day was spent in making preparation and issuing orders and equipment. At 10.15 p.m. the battalion marched out of Fresnoy to take up a position for attack in a sunken road in Valley Hassard north-east of Bohain.

Riqueval Wood had held up the advance of the 46th Division for nearly a week. Woods are awkward places to capture and easy places to fortify. The Germans were holding on to Riqueval Wood like grim death ; it was defended by brave and desperate men who determined that only grim death should take it from their hands. It was full of machine-gun nests, strong posts, trenches and wire. It was the kind of place which an unimaginative general might attack and lose ten thousand men before breakfast. The 5th Leicesters and the Stafford Brigade had attempted to enter the wood without success. General Boyd, who was by no means an unimaginative general, decided that an attack should be made on the north flank, and that the wood should be taken by a turning movement rather than a frontal attack. The objective of the 46th Division was the Bohain-Wassigny Road from the north-east corner of Riqueval Wood to the village of Andigny-les-Fermes. The direction of the advance was almost due south and the hamlet of Regnicourt was in the centre of the objective.

The 4th battalion reached the sunken road in the Valley Hassard in the early hours of October 17th. The night was dark and there was no opportunity to reconnoitre the ground. Zero hour was 5.20 a.m., and the jumping-off place was one hundred yards in front of the road, as it was expected the enemy would shell the road as soon as the attack began. Punctually to the moment the companies advanced. The Lincolns were the left of the line, then the 4th Leicesters ; the Sherwood Brigade was on the right. The day was fine, but there was a thick fog ; observation was limited to a few yards. When the barrage began, which included a number of smoke shells, observation finished altogether and the troops had to grope their way forward as best they could and trust to luck and compass to keep direction. The barrage, instead of coming from guns in rear of the advancing troops, came from the right flank opposite Riqueval Wood, where a battalion of Staffords worked dummy men and dummy tanks to deceive the enemy and attract his barrage, thus giving the attacking troops a better chance. A barrage from a flank was an innovation ; the troops were not used to shells coming across their front at right angles, with the result that there was some confusion. It was difficult to tell whether they were our own shells or the enemy's. Some men got too far forward and were knocked over by their own barrage, and it was not until the barrage had moved forward several times that the infantry got used to it and understood how it worked, but in the meantime they had suffered considerable casualties from it.

From their jumping-off place the battalion moved up a slope for a few hundred yards ; halfway up they came across a thin line of wire protecting shallow rifle pits fifty yards apart ; this obstacle gave them no trouble and they pushed on to the top of the ridge where they found a five-foot deep trench which had been hastily dug. Luckily this trench turned in a southerly direction so they could enfilade it. This offered little resistance, but machine-gun bullets were coming far too thickly through the fog, the enemy were shelling, and our own barrage was still difficult to follow. The fog of war was indeed thick ; five yards ahead was as much as anyone could see. It was most difficult to keep direction, but on the battalion groped in spite of casualties, and before noon the objective, the Bohain-Wassigny Road, was reached. This was crossed and everyone began to dig in. Men of many different regiments appeared at this point ; 5th Lincolns, from the left, Loyal North Lancs, Cameron Highlanders, and Black Watch from the 1st Division who were attacking still further on the left, Sherwoods from the right. All began busily to dig. These men knew something of attacks ; they also knew something about counter-attacks and they were not going to be caught unprepared.

The fog, which had caused so much mixing up of the attacking troops, had been a real godsend to them. Through it they had been able to rush the forward defences before the enemy realised from which direction they were being attacked. Andigny-les-Fermes standing on the high ground at the left of the divisional front had been rushed by the Loyal North Lancashires of the 1st Division. Regnicourt, a strongly defended hamlet in the centre of the objective, had fallen with three hundred prisoners to Captain H. F. Papprill and "D" Company. Both places had put up a stiff fight and caused many casualties, but without the fog they would have been a much tougher proposition. The fog, however, had been a great hindrance to the moppers-up. The enemy had left machine-gun nests intact hidden away in smoke and cloud, and when the sun broke through the attackers found themselves being shot at from behind. This was most uncomfortable, but the situation was taken in hand by tanks and gallant parties of infantry, and finally all resistance in rear was quelled. The gunners had helped very considerably in the attack not only with the barrage, but certain field guns were allotted to battalion commanders who rushed them forward to assist the infantry. They were of great assistance in firing at short range over open sights on any strong point or machine-gun nest which was holding up the advance, and they gave great confidence to the assaulting troops.

This was the last pitched battle in which the 46th Division took part. It was a brilliant success. All objectives were taken. The enemy were forced to evacuate Riqueval Wood without inflicting heavy losses on the division. Touch was obtained with the French, who were attacking at the same time towards Mennevet, and on the 18th the allied advance was being continued towards Wassigny. Co-operation with the 1st and 6th Divisions fighting on the left of the 46th had been excellent throughout.

There had been casualties ; there always are, battles cannot be won without casualties. Such is victory. The bands play, the bayonets glisten in the sunlight, the victorious general takes the salute, Atkins sticks his chest out and turns his head and eyes sharply to the right, enjoined by the sergeant-major to "put a jerk into it." But no sergeant-major on earth can put a jerk into the poor ragged bundles of khaki and field-grey that lie so still in the fields between Valley Hassard and Regnicourt. Such is victory.

One day in the nineties a boy baby was born of humble parents in a Lancashire manufacturing town. He had red hair, and though his surname was Gardner everybody quite naturally called him "Ginger." He grew up a fine healthy lad and became a dyer's labourer. War broke out; Ginger promptly pulled off his overalls and became a private soldier. Ginger took soldiering seriously; he was soon a non-commissioned officer and at last was recommended for a commission. In due course he joined the 4th Leicesters as a Second-Lieutenant and was posted to "A" Company. "A" Company were used to highly efficient officers but they wondered what they had got when this new red-headed subaltern arrived. They very soon found out. If there was any particularly nasty and unpleasant little thing to be done in No Man's Land Ginger was on the job. He was willing, efficient, happy, the personification of energy, and with a pleasant way of doing things. The men liked him, the officers had a genuine affection for him, and his Company Commander, Captain A. B. Pick, did not like to be without him. As luck would have it "Ginger" was on leave for the Bellenglise fight and did not arrive at the transport lines until the evening of October 3rd, the day of the Battle of Ramicourt. Most subalterns returning from leave at that hour would have had a whisky-and-soda with the quartermaster, and as the transport had left for the line would have borrowed a couple of blankets, slept the sleep of the just, and gone quietly up the line the next morning with a guide. That was the proper way of doing things, but it wasn't Ginger's way. He heard there was a show on, that his company was in the line. Possibly his platoon were hanging on somewhere by the skin of their teeth; possibly his company commander had a job for him. Ginger did not stop long at the transport lines; off he went in the darkness to find his company. How many miles he walked that night, or how many times he lost his way no one will ever know, but before dawn he poked his ginger head into Pick's dug-out and reported for duty. The rest of the night and following day he spent hanging on to a railway bank with his platoon pumping lead into counter-attacks. Later, on October 9th, he outflanked some enemy machine-guns who were holding up the advance to Fresnoy. He was always on the spot when he was wanted, full of sense, full of guts, and with a meticulous regard for duty. Andigny was his last fight. His platoon got into the barrage during the advance and he was mortally wounded, and died at the dressing station at Valley Hassard, tended by the gallant Captain Brown, R.A.M.C., the battalion's M.O. "Ginger" Gardner was a born fighting man and, what is more, a born leader of the type that both the regiment and the British Army could ill afford to lose.

On the evening of October 17th the battalion was relieved in the front line by the 5th Leicestershires, and moved back to the old German front line where the night was spent.

Next day the battalion moved back to billets in Fresnoy and marched past the divisional general and brigadier en route.

CHAPTER XLIII

THE LAST CHAPTER

THE battalion remained in billets at Fresnoy from October 18th to November 1st. The billets were good, though the Germans had knocked some of them about wantonly. They thought nothing of smashing all the biggest mirrors (not that it brought them any luck), breaking up any odd pianos they found, ransacking cupboards and wardrobes and scattering the contents broadcast. Quite unworthy actions for a foe who had put up such a long and stout resistance. However, at least one piano was rescued, and because language is national but music international, some of the subalterns found that the local Aphrodites took more notice if they said it with music.

Fresnoy Le Grand did not belie its name ; the battalion had a great time there. Plenty of time was given for cleaning and baths. New drafts arrived. Companies were reorganised and brought up to strength. Many of the men slightly wounded at Bellenglise and Ramicourt came back to the battalion. There was a Divisional Church Parade with its concomitant spitting and polishing, but a feeling of thankfulness pervaded the service. The valley of the shadow of death was quite definitely getting a brighter and more healthy place. The weather was beautiful, October at its best, an exhilarating nip in the morning air, bright sunshine at midday, a pleasant shimmering mist as the sun went to bed. The fire was welcome in the billet, and the villagers did all they could to be friendly and kind. The mornings were spent in various kinds of training and on the range, the afternoons in recreational training, which is, being interpreted, "football."

On October 26th the battalion formed part of the guard of honour to a French divisional commander who presented the Croix de Guerre to various officers and N.C.O.'s who were duly gratified, but who were glad when the ceremony was over.

On October 31st the C.O. inspected the battalion in the afternoon ; this was ominous. Life at Fresnoy had been good, a few bombs by night, a shell or two by day, but after all there was still a war on and the division could not be out of it for long. So next day at 3 p.m., having bid many fond farewells to the fair ones of the village, the battalion formed fours and marched out of Fresnoy and on to billets at Busigny seven miles north-east.

After a day at Busigny the battalion marched three miles east to Molain and spent the night under canvas. Not much fun under canvas in November, especially as the weather was breaking up and getting cold and wet. Still, no one minded much ; everybody knew that the Boche was now properly on the run ; the Allies were moving miles eastward daily ; Turkey and Bulgaria had thrown up the sponge ; Austria no longer counted. It was only a case of pushing on and getting the job finished. The morale of the troops was wonderful. On November 4th the battalion marched through Ribeauville to Mazingheim where they relieved the Camerons of the 1st Division in the line. Next day they pushed joyfully east to La Groise where the Staffords passed through them. By the evening of the 6th they had marched, via Prisches, to Cartignies a good seven miles. The Germans had only just left and were still firing machine-guns from the hills nearby. The civilians were mad with excitement and delight and gave the battalion a great welcome and they stayed up all night with the town well lit up. The troops found billets, but next day the advance continued and the battalion was in support to the brigade marching on Avesnes, two companies being attached to the 5th Leicestershires.

Cavalry covered the advance ; the roads were bad and in many places impassable owing to being blown up by mines left by the enemy. Tracks and fields often had to be used and this was heavy going for transport and guns in bad weather. The roads were strewn with German transport ; men and horses lay in heaps ; our guns had played havoc with them in their retreat.

On November the 10th the battalion marched seven miles east to Sains Du Nord. The civilians were delighted. The Germans had only left eight hours before. The battalion was billeted in the village school ; the H.Q. of one company was at the schoolmaster's house. The schoolmaster's daughter, who had a good voice, sang for the first time for four years. She brought out strings of British and French flags, which she had kept hidden away in a box since the Germans came, and hung them from the windows into the street—altogether it was a good Sunday evening.

Then at the eleventh hour of the eleventh day of the eleventh month the fire of the guns died away and Battalion H.Q. received a wire from brigade to say hostilities were to cease at 11.00. The battalion took over an outpost line east of Sains Du Nord, two companies on outpost, two in support. An armistice had been signed. The end of the war had come.

There was no wild excitement ; a spirit of extreme thankfulness prevailed. Everyone was tired, everyone wanted a rest. Victory had come but it had come quietly. It was a time to rest and be thankful.

On November 13th the battalion moved to billets in Avesnelles and on the 14th to billets at Bousies where it remained till

February 24th, 1919. Life at Bousies was pleasant. Training and salvaging in the mornings, football and sports in the afternoons.

On December 1st the battalion marched to Landrecies to see His Majesty the King. It was an informal visit and the troops and civilians cheered King George to the echo. It was the same King who had reviewed the battalion at Luton Hoo four years before ; it was the same battalion in name and spirit only ; few of the original members had come through the war unscathed.

The King smiles, the victorious troops raise cheer after cheer.

The curtain falls. Thank God, for some, at least, the tragedy has a happy ending.

R. I. P.

From Kemmel Hill to Bellenglise, from Lens to Dickebushe,
Through all the gory gamut, from "inspection" unto "push."
In perils oft, in weariness, in trenches, and in rum,
They waged the war to end all war until Thy Kingdom come.

From laughter loud to dark despair, from "leave" to "listening post,"
From lusty life at zero hour to puking up the ghost,
In agony and bloody sweat they paid the utmost sum,
To sleep the sleep that ends all sleep until Thy Kingdom come.

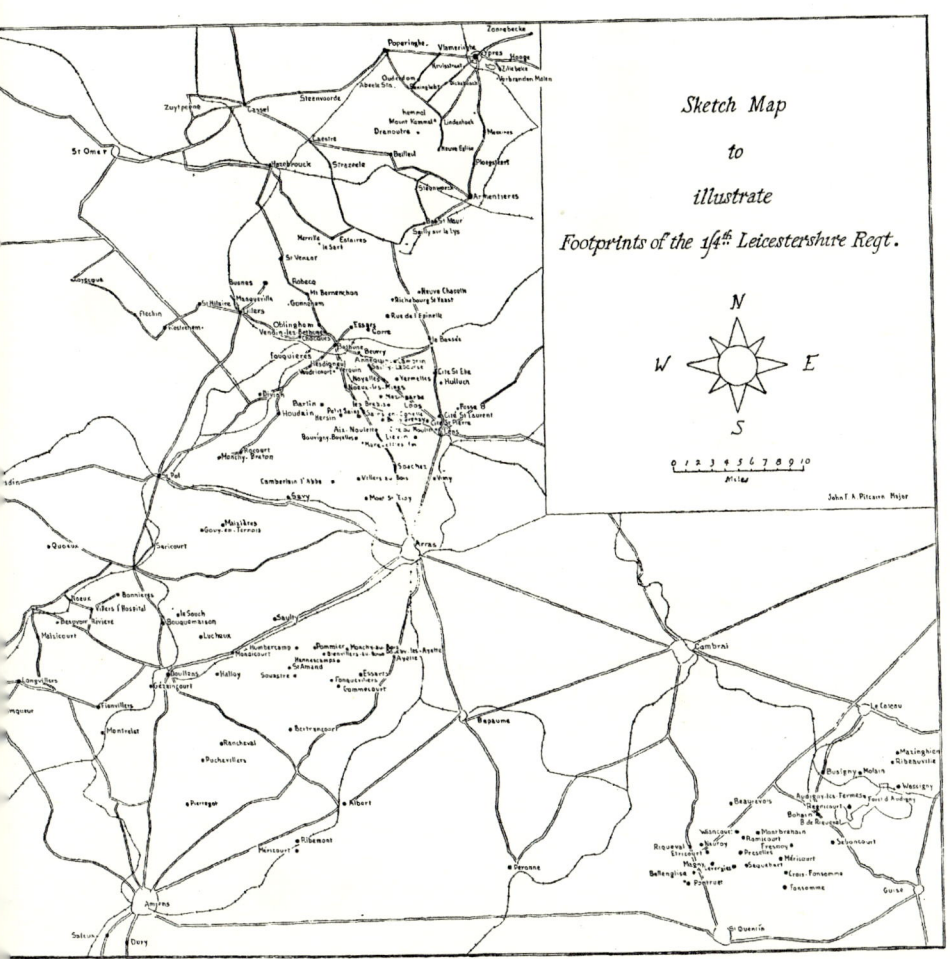

Sketch Map

to

illustrate

Footprints of the 1/4th Leicestershire Regt.

John F. A. Pitcairn, Major

Printed in the United Kingdom
by Lightning Source UK Ltd.
113567UKS00001B/409-411